AF609223

A Treatyse of Fysshynge wyth an Angle

by Dame Juliana Berners

and

Barker's Delight: Or, The Art of Angling

by Thomas Barker

Contents

A
TREATYSE OF FYSSHYNGE WYTH AN ANGLE

Here beginneth a
Treatyse of Fysshynge wyth an Angle.

Salomon in his parables sayeth that a good spyrite maketh a flouring age that is a fayre age and a longe. And sythe it is so, I aske this question, whiche be the meanes and the causes that enduce a man into a mery spyryte? Truely to my best discretion it semeth good disportes and honest games in whom a man joyeth without any repentaunce after. Then foloweth it that good disportes and honest games: be cause of mannes fayre age and longe lyfe. And therfore nowe we wyll I chose of foure good dysportes and honest games, that is to wete of Haukyng, Huntyng, and fyshyng, and for foulyng. The best to my discrecion whiche is fyshying called anglyng with a rod, and a lyne, and an hoke, and therof to treat as my symple wyt may suffyse, both for the sayd reason of Salomon, & also for the reason that reason maketh in this wyse.

Si tibi deficiant medici, medici tibi fiant. Hec tria,

mens leta, labor, et moderata dieta.

Ye shall vnderstande that this is for to say, if a man lackes leche or medicine, he shall make thre thynges his medicine and he shall neuer need moe. The first of them is a mery thought. The seconde is a labour not outragious. The third is diet mesurable. The first if a man will euer more be in mery thought and haue a glad spyrite, he must eschew all contrarious company and all places of debate where he myght haue any occasions of melancholy, & if he wyll haue a labour not outragious: he must then ordeyne hym to his hartes ease, and plesaunce without study, pensyfnes of trauayle, a mery occupacion whiche may reioyce his harte, and in which his spirites may haue a mery delyte. And if he will be dieted measurably he must eschewe all places of ryot, whiche is cause of surfet and of syckenesse, and he must drawe hym to places of swete ayre and hungry, and eate nouryshable meates and disyrable also.

As now than wyll I descryue the sayd disportes and games to fynde the beste of them as berely as I can, all be it that the ryght noble and full worthy prynce Duke of Yorke late called mayster of the game, hath discryued the mirthes of huntyng like as I thinke to discryue of it and of al other. For huntyng as to mine intent is to laborous. For the hunter must alway tunne and folowe his houndes traueling and sweting ful sore. He bloweth till his lyppes blyster. And whan he weneth it be a hare: full oft it is an hedgehogge. Thus he chaseth and woteth not what. He commeth home at euen rayne beten, pycked, and his clothes torn, wete shod and all myrde. Some hounds lost, some surbate. Suche greues and many others happeth vnto the hunter, whiche for displeasaunce of them that loue it, I dare not reporte. Thus truly me semeth that this is not the best disporte & game of the said foure.

The disport & game of Hauking is laborous & noyus also as me semeth. for as often the faukener leseth his haukes, as the hunter his houndes, than is his game & disporte gone, often cryeth & whysteleth til he be ryght euill a thrust. His hauke taketh a bow & list not ones on him to regarde. Whan he would haue her to fle: than will she bath. With misfeeding she shall haue ye frounce ye rie ye cray & many other sicknesses y^t^ bringeth them to souse. Thus by profe this is not the best disporte & game of the sayd foure.

The disport and game of foulyng me semeth moste symplest. For in the wynter season the fouler speedeth not, but in the hardest and coldest of the wether whiche is greuous for whan he would go to his ginnes he may not for colde. Many a gin & many a snare he maketh, yet sorely doth he fare, at morne tide in ye dells he is welshod vnto his taile. Many other such I could tel but dred of maugre maketh me to leue.

Thus me semeth that huntyng and haukyng, and also foulyng, ben so laborous & greuous, that none of them may perfourme nor be very meane to enduce a man to a mery spyryte whiche is cause of thys longe lyfe according vnto the sayd parable of Salomon. Doubtles then foloweth it that it muste needes be the disport of fyshyng with an angle. For all other maner of fysshynge is also laborous and greuous, often makyng of folkes ful were and colde which many tymes hath ne seen cause of greate infirmities, but the angler maye haue no colde nor dysease nor angre, but yf he be causer hym selfe, for he maye not lose at the mooste but a lyne or an hooke: of which he may haue store plentye of hys owne makynge, as thys simple treatyse shall teache hym. So then hys losse is not greuous, and other greefes maye he not haue sauynge but yf any fysshe break away after y^t^ he is taken on the hooke, or els y^t^ he catch nought whyche is not greuous, for yf he fayle of one he maye not fayle of an other, yf he doth as thys treatyse teacheth, but if there be nought in the water, and yet as the least he hath his holsome walke and mery at his ease, sweet ayre of the sweet sauour of the medow floures that maketh him hungry. He heareth the melodious armony of foules. He seeth the yonge swans, herons, duckes, cootes, and many other foules with their broodes, whyche me semeth better then all the noyse of houndes, the blastes of hornes, & the scry of foules, that hunters, faukeners, & foulers can make. And if the angler take fyshe: surely then is there no man meryer then he is in his spirite. And who so wyl vse thys game of anglyng: he muste ryse early, which is profytable to man in this wyse. That is to wete, most to to the health of hys soule. For it that cause hym to be holy, & to the helth of his body for that it shal cause him to be whole. Also to the encrease of hys gooddes, for it shall make hym ryche; as the olde Englysh prouerbe sayth in this wyse. W.o so wyll ryse early, shalbe holy, helthy, & happy. Thus haue I proued in myne entent that the disporte and game of angling: is the very meane and cause that enduceth a man into a mery spy-rite, Which after the sayd parable of Salomon and the sayd doctryne and the Physicke maketh a stourynge age and a long, and therefore to all you that ben vertuous gentyll and fre borne, I wryte & make this simple tretise folowing by the which ye may haue the full craft of angling to disport you at your lust to then-tent that your age m[a]y the more floure, and the more longer endure.

If ye wyl be crafty in angling, ye must first learne to make your harneys, that is to wete your rod, your lines of diuers colours, after that you must know how ye shall angle, in what place of the water, how depe and what time of the daye, for what maner of fysshe, in what wether, how many impedimentes there bene of fysshyng that is called anglyng, and in specially wyth what baytes to euery dyuers fyshhe, in euery moneth of the yeare. How ye shall make your baytes breed, where ye shal finde them, and how ye shall fynd them, and how ye shall kepe them and for the moost crafty thyng, how you shall make your hookes of stele and of osmonde. Some for the dub and some for the flote on the ground.

And howe you shall make your rod craftely, here I shall teache you, ye shall cut betweene Michelmas & Candelmas a fayre staffe of a fadome and a halfe longe and arme great of hasyll, wyllowe or aspe, and breath hym in a hote ouen, and set hym euen. Then let hym coole and drye a moneth, take then and frete hym fast wyth a cokshote cord, and bynde it to a fourme of an euen square great tre. Then take a plummer wyer that is euen and strayght, and sharpe at the one ende, and heate the sharpe ende in a charcole fyre tyll it be hote, and bren the staffe therewith through, euer streyght in the pith at both endes tyll they mete, and after that bren him in the nether end with a byrde broche, and with other broches eche greater then other and euer the greatest the last, so that ye make your hole aye taper wyse. Then let hym lye styl and kele two dayes, vnfrete hym then and let hym dry in a house roofe, in the smoke tyll he be through drye[. I]n the same season take a fayre yerde of grene hasell, and bathe it euen & strayght and let it dry with the staffe and when they ben drye make the yerde mete vnto the hole in the staffe vnto half the length of the staffe, and to perfourme that other halfe of the crop, take a fayre shote of blacke thorne, crab tree medler or els of Ienepre cut in the same season, and well bethed, and streyght, and set them together fetely, so that the crop may iustly enter all into the sayde hole. Then shaue your staffe and make hym capre waye, then vyrell the staffe at both endes with long hoopes of yron or larton, in the clennest wyse, a pyke in the nether ende fastened with a rennyng vyce, to take in and out your crop. Then set your crop an handfull within the ouer ende of your staffe, in suche wyse that it be as bygge there as in any other place aboue, then arme your crop at the ouer ende downe to the fret with a lyne of syx heates, and double the lyne and frete it fast in the toppe with a bowe to fasten on your lyne. And thus shall ye make you a rod so pryuy that ye may walke there with, and there wyll neuer any man wete what thyng ye go about. It wyll be very lyght & nymble to fyshe with at your pleasure, & for the more redynes, lo here a fygure therof in example.

After ye haue thus made youre rodde: ye muste learne for to colour your lynes of heare in this wyse. First ye must take of a whyte horse tayle the longest heare and fayrest that ye can fynde, and euer the rounder that it be: the better it is. Departe it in syxe partes, & euery part ye shall colour by him selfe in diuers colours as yelowe, grene, browne, tawny, russet, & duske coloure. And for to make good greene coloures on your heare, ye shal do take smale ale a quarte, and put it into a litle pan and put therto halfe a pounde of Alum, and put therto your heate and let it boyle softly halfe an houre. Than take out your heare and let it drye, than take a pottell of fayre water and put it in a pan and put therin two handes full of Wyxene, and presse it with a tyle stone, and let it boyle softly the space of an houre. And whan it is yelowe on the scum: put therein your heare, with halfe a pounde of coperose beaten in pouder, and lette it boyle halfe a myle waye. And than set it downe and let it kele fyue or syxe houres. Than take out the heate and drie it, and it is than the fynest greene that is possible to be had for the water. And euer the more that ye put therto of cuperose the better it will be, or elles in the stede of it Vert-grese.

And an other way may ye make a bryghter greene, as thus. Lette wod your heare in a wodden fat of lyght plunket colour and than set hym in olde or wyxen lyke as I haue shewed you before, sauyng ye shall not putte therin neyther coperose or vertegrees.

For to make your heare seme yelowe, dight it with Alum as I haue sayde before, and after that with oldes or Wyxen without coperose or vertgrece.

An other yelowe ye shall make thus. Take smale ale & pottle, and stampe thre handfull of walnut leues & put it together, and put in your heare tyll that it be as deep as ye wyll haue it.

For to make russet heare. Take a pynte of strong lyes & a half pound of soote, and a lytle iuce of walnut leues and a quart of Alum, & put them all together in a pan, and boile them wel, and whan it is colde: put in your heare till it be as darcke as ye wyll haue it.

For to make a browne coloure. Take a pounde of soote & a quarte of ale, and seeth wyth as many walnut leues as ye may, and whan they be blacke set it from the fyre, and put therin heare & let it lye styll til it be as browne as ye wyll haue it.

For to make an other browne. Take strong ale, and soote and tempre them together and put there to your heare two dayes and two nyghtes, and it shal be a ryght good coloure.

For to make a tawny coloure. Take lyme and water & put them together, and also put your heare therin foure or fyue houres. Than take it out and put it into a tanner sole one daye and it shal be as fine a tawny coloure as any nedeth to our purpose.

The sixe parte of your heare ye wall kepe styl white for lines, for the double hooke to fysshe for the troute & graylynge, and for small lynes for to lye for the roche & the Dase.

Whan your heare is thus coloured: ye must know for whiche waters and for which seasons they shall serue. The greene colour in all cleare waters from Apryl unto September. The yelow colour in euery clere water, from Se[p]tembre to Nouembre for it is lyke to the wedes and other maner of grasse whyche groweth in the waters and ryuers whan they be broken.

The russet colour serueth al the wynter vnto the ende of Apryll, as well in ryuers as in pooles, or lakes.

The browne colour, serueth for that water that is black dedish in ryuers or other waters. Then tawny colour, for these waters that ben hethy or morysh.

Now must ye make your lynes, in this wyse. Fyrst looke ye haue an instrument lyke vnto this fygure portrayed folowyng. Than take your heare and cut of the ende an handfull large or more. For it is neyther stronge nor sure. Than turne the top to the tayle, euery one like much and departe it into three partes. Than knyt euerye parte at one ende by hym selfe, and at the other ende knytte all three together. And than put the same ende in that other ende of your instrument that hath but one clyft. And than set that other ende fast with the wedge foure fyngers in all shorter than your heare. Than twyne euery warpe one waye, and lyke muche, and fast them in the clyftes alyke streyght. Take that out at that other ende, & than twyne it that waye that it wyll desyre enough. Than strayne it a lytle and knyt it for vndoyng and that is good. And for to knowe howe to make your instrument: lo here a fygure. And it shalbe made of tree, sauyng the bolte vnderneth, whiche shalbe of yron.

So whan you haue as many of the lynkes as ye suppose wil suffyse for the length of a lyne: than must ye knyt them together with a water knot, or els a duches knot, and when your knot is knyt: cut of the voyte short endes a straw bred fro the knot. Thus shall your lynes be fayre and fyne, and also right sure for any maner of fysshe.

Ye shall vnderstande, that the moste subtill and hardest craft in makyng your harneys, is for to make your hookes. For whose makyng ye must haue feete toles thyn and sharpe and small beaten, a semy clam of yron, a bender, a payre of long and small tones, and an harde knyfe somedely thyke and an anuylde, and a lytle hamner.

And for small fysshe, ye shall make your hookes of the smallest quarell nedilles that ye can fynde of stele, and in this wyse ye shall put the quarell in a read charcole fyre, tyll it be of the same coloure that the fyre is. Than take hym out and let hym kele, and ye shall fynde hym well allayed for to fyle. Than rayse the barde with your knyfe, and make the poynt sharpe. Than alay him agayne or els he will breake in the bendyng. Than bende hym lyke to the bende accordyng to the purpose. And greater hookes ye shall make in the same wyse of great nedles, as broderers nedelles, or taylers, or shoomakers nedles, spere pointes of shoomakers nailes, in especiall the best for greate fysshe, and loke that they bend at the poynt whan they ben assayed, for els they be not good. whan the hoke is bended bete the hinder ende abrode, and fyle it smothe for fretting of the lyne. Than put it into the fyre agayne, & geue it an easy read heate. Than sodonly quenche it in water, and it wyll be harde and strong. And for to haue knowledge in your instruments: loe they be here in figure portrayed.

Hamer, Knyfe Pynsops, Clame, Wedge, Fyle, Wrest, & Inuelde.

When ye haue made your hookes: then must ye set them on your lynes accordyng in greatnes and strength in this wyse, ye shall take small read sylke, and if it be for a great hooke then dowble it not, twyned. And els for small hookes let it be syngle, and therewith frete thycke the lyne there as the one ende of your hooke shall fyt a strawe breade. Then set there your hooke and freete him with the same threde the two partes of the length that shalbe fret in all. And when ye come to the thyrde part: then turne the ende of your lyne agayne vpon the fret double, and frete it so double at the other thyrde parte, then put your threde in at the hole twyse or thryse, and let it goe eche tyme round aboute the yerde of your hooke, then were the hole and drawe tyll it be faste, and looke that youre lyne lye euermore within your hookes, and not without, then cut of the lynes ende and the threde, as nyghe as ye may sauyng the frete.
So ye knowe with howe great hookes ye shall angle to euery fysshe now I wyll tell you with howe many heares ye shall angle to euery fysshe. Fyrst for the Menowe with a lyne of one heare. For the waryng roche, the bleke, the Gogyn and the Ruf with a lyne of two heares, for the Darse and the great Roche with a lyne

of thre heares. For the Perche with Flounder and Bremer with foure heares. For the Cheuyn chubbe, the Breme, the Tenche, and the Eele with six heares. For the Troute, graylyng barbell & the great cheuyn: with nyne heares. For the greate [troute] with twelve heares. For the Samon with fyftene heares, and for the pyke with a chalke lyne made browne with youre browne coloure aforesayde armed with a lyne as ye shall heare hereafter whan I speake of the pyke. Your lynes must be plummed with lead. And ye shall wete that the next plumbe to the hooke, shalbe therfro a large foote and more, and euery plumbe a quantitie vnto the greatnes of the lyne. There be the maner of plumbes for a grounde lyne rennyng. And for the flote set vpon the ground lyne lyeng .x. plumbes ioynyng all together on the ground line rennyng nyne or ten small. The flote plumbe shal be heuy that the first plucke of any fysshe may pull it downe into the water, and make your plumbes round and smothe, y[t] they stick not on stones or weedes, and for the more vnderstandyng, lo here be they in fygures.

The ground lyne, rennyng and lyeng.

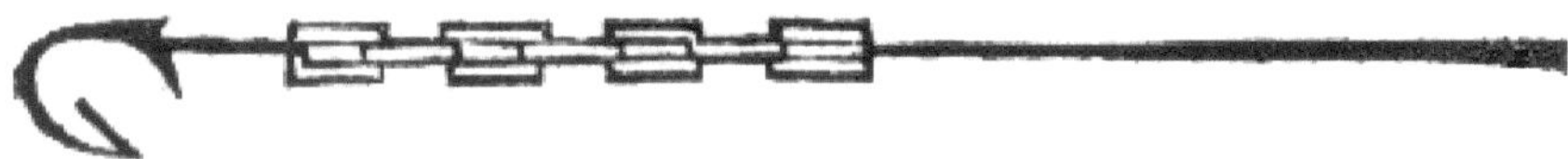

The Flote lyne, and the lyne for Perche or Tenche.

The lyne for a pyke, plumbe, corke, and armed with wire.

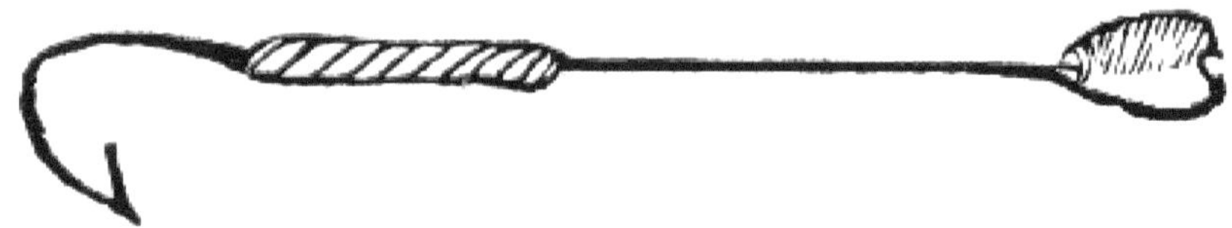

Then shall ye make your flotes in this wyse. Take a fayre corke that is clene wtout any holes and bore it through with a small bore yron, and put therin a pen iust and streyght, euermore note the greater pen, and the greater hole. Than shape it great in the middes, and smal at both endes, and specially sharpe in the nether ende, and lyke vnto the fygures folowyng and make them smothe on a grydyng stone or on a tyle stone, and looke that floote for one heare be no more then a pease, for two heares as a beane, for twelue heares as a walnut, and so euery lyne must haue accordyng to his porcion.

All maner lynes that be not for the grounde must haue flotes, and the rennyng ground lyne must haue a flote, the lyeng ground lyne must haue a flote.

NOw I haue lerned you to make all your harneys. Here I wyll tell you how ye shall angle.

Ye shall understande that there is syxe maner of anglyng. That one is at the ground for the troute and other fysshe. An other is at the grounde at an arche or a stange, where it ebbeth and floweth: for bleke, roche, and Darse. The thirde is with a flote for all maner of fysshe. The fourth with a menow for the Troute, without plumbe or flote. The Fyfth is rennyng in the same for the Roche and darse, with one or to heares and a flye. The syxte is a dubbed hooke, for the Troute or Graylyng. And for the fyrst and pryncipall poynt in anglyng: kepe the euer from the water for the syght of the fysshe, eyther ferre vpon the lande, or els behynde a bushe that the fyshe se you not. For if they doo: they wyll not byte. And looke that y[e] shadowe not the water as much as ye maye. For it is that thyng that wyll sone fraye the fyshe. And if a fysshe be a frayde: he wyll not byte long after. For all maner of fysshe that fede by the grounde ye shall angle for them to the bottome, so that your hooke shall renne, or lye on the grounde. And for all other fysshe, that fedeth aboue: ye shall angle for them in the mides of the water, or somdely beneth, or som dele aboue, for euer the greater fysshe: the nerer he lyeth to the botome of the water. And euer the smaler fysshe the more he swymmeth aboue. The thyrde good poynte is whan the fysshe byteth that ye be not to hasty to smyte, nor to late. For ye must abyde tyll ye suppose that the bayte be fer in the mouthe of the fysshe and then abyde no lenger, and this is for the ground. And for the floote, when ye se it pulled softly vnder the water, or eis caryed softly vpon the water, then smite. And looke that ye neuer ouersmite the strength of your lyne for breakyng. And if it fortune you to smyte a great fyshhe with a small harneys, then ye must lede hym in the water, and labour him there tyll he be drowned and overcome. Then take him as well as ye can or may, and euer be ware that ye holde not ouer the strength of your lyne. And as much as ye may let him not come out of your lines ende streyght from you but kepe him euer vnder the rod, and euermore holde him streight so that your lyne may susteyne and beare his leapes and his plunges with the helpe of your crop and of your hand.

Here I wyll declare vnto you, in what place of the water ye shall angle, ye shall angle in a poole or in a landing water in euery place where it is any thing deepe.

There is no great choyse of any place where it is any thyng depe in a poole. For it is but a pryson vnto all fysshes & therfore it is the lesse maistry to take them. But in a riuer, ye shall angle in euery place where it is depe and clere by the ground: as grauell or clay without mud or wedes, and in espe-ciall if that there be a maner whyrlyng of water or a couert. As an holowe banke or great rootes of trees, or long weedes floting aboue the waters where as the fysshe may couer and hyde them self at certayne tymes when they lyst. Also it is good for to angle in depe styffe streames, and also in vallays of water and weares, and in flode gates or myll pyttes.

And at the banke, and where the streame renneth nyghe therby, and is depe and clere by the grounde and in any other places where ye may se any fysshe haue any feding.

As now shall ye wyt, what tyme of the day ye shall an-gle. From the begynning of Maye vntill it be September: the byting tyme is early in the morow from four of the clocke vnto eyght of the clocke, at after none from foure to eyght also, but not so good as in the mornyng, and if it be a colde wynde and a lowryng day, it is muche better than a cleere daye. Also many poole fysshes will byte best in the morne tyde.

And if ye se in any tyme of the day the Troute or greylyng lepe angle to him with a dub according to the same moneth. And where the water ebbeth and floweth: the fish wyll byte in some place at the ebbe and in some place at the flud after they haue restyng behynde stanges, and arches of brydges, and other suche maner places.

Here shal ye wete in what maner of wether ye shal angle in, as I sayd before in a darke louryng daye whan the winde bloweth softly. And in sommer season whan it is brenning hote, than it is naught. From Septembre vnto Apryll, in a fayre sunny daye it is ryght good to angle: and yf the wynde in that season haue any parte of the Oryent wether: than it is naught, and whan it is great wynde whan it snoweth, rayneth, or hayleth, or is a great tempest, as thunder or lyghtnynge or a swoly hote wether: than it is nought for to angle.

Ye shall now wit that there be twelue maner of impedymentes whiche cause a man to take no fysshe, without other comyn that may casually hap. The fyrst is if your harneis be not mete, nor fetely made. The second is, if your baytes be not good nor fyne. The third is if that ye angle not in byting tyme. The fourth is if the fysshe be frayde with the syght of a man. The fyft if that the water be ve[r]y thycke, whyte or read of any floude late fallen. The syxt if the fysshe stere not for colde. The seuenth, if that the wether be hote. The eyght, if it rayne. The .ix. if it hayle or snowe. The .x. if it be tempest. The .xi. if it be great wynde. The .xii. if the wynde be in the east, and that is worste. For commonly neyther wynter nor somer the fysshe wyl not byte than. The west and the north wynde ben good, but the south is best.

And nowe I haue told you howe to make your harneys, and howe ye shall fysshe therewith in all poyntes: reason wyll that ye knowe with what baytes ye shall angle to euery maner of fysshe in euery moneth of the yere whiche is all the effect of the craft. And without whiche baytes: knowen well by you, all your other crafte here toforne auayleth you not to purpose. For ye cannot brynge a hooke into a fysshe mouthe withoute a bayte, whiche baytes for euery maner of fysshe, and for euery moneth here foloweth in this wyse.

As now because that the Samon is more statelye fysshe that any man maye angle to in fresshe water: Therfore I purpose to begyn at hym.

The Samon is a gentyll fysshe, but he is cumberous for to take. For commonly he is but in depe places of great ryuers, and for the moste part he holdeth him in the myddes of it, that a man may not come at hym. And he is in season from Marche vnto Michelmas. In whiche season ye shall angle to hym with these baytes whan ye may get them. First with a red worme in the begynnyng and endyng of the season, and also with a grub that breedeth in a dunghill, and especially with a souerayne bayte that bredeth in a water docke. And he bydeth not at the ground but at the floote, also ye may take hym, but it is seldome seene with a grub at such tymes as whan he lepeth, in lyke fourme and maner as ye do take a Troute or a Gralyng, and these ben well proued baytes for the Samon.

The Troute for because he is a right deynteous fisshe and also feruent bitter, we shall speake next of hym. He is in season fro Marcshe vnto Mychelmas. He is on clene grauell grounde, and in a streame, ye may angle to hym at all tymes with a ground lyne, lying or rennyng, sauing only in leapyng time, and than with a dubbe. And erly with a rennyng grounde lyne, and forth on the daye with a flote line.

Ye shal angle to hym in Marche with a menow hanged on your hooke by the nethernes without floote or plumbe drawyng vp and downe in the streme tyll ye feele him fast. In the same tyme angle to him with ground lynes, and with a red worme for the moste sure. In Aprill take the same baytes and also Iuneba, otherwyse named .vii. eyes, & also the canker that breedeth in a great tre & the red snayle.

In May take the stone flye & the bobbe vnder the cow torde & the sylk worm & the bayte y^t bredeth on a ferne lefe.

In Iune take a red worme & nip of the head and a codworme before vpon the hoke. In Iuly take the great red worme & the codworme together. In August take a flesh flye, and the great red worme, and the fat of the bakon, & bynde them together about the hoke. In Septembre take the read worme and the menow. In October take the same, for they be special for the trout at al tymes of the yere. From Apryll tyll September the troute lepeth than angle to hym with a dubbed hoke accordyng to the moneth whiche dubbed hookes ye shall fynde at the ende of this tratyse, and the monethes with them.

The Grayling by an other name called Umbre is a ryght delcious fysshe to mannis mouthe, and ye may take him as ye do the Troute, and these ben his baytes. In Marche & in Apryll the read worme. In May the greene worme, a lytle braised worme, the docke canker and the haut.orne worme. In Iune the bayte that breedeth betwene the tree and the barke of an Oke. In Iuly a bayte that bredeth on a ferne lefe and a great red worm and nyp of the head and put it on your hooke, and a cod worme before, in August the read worme and a Docke worme, and all the yere after a read worme.

The Barbell is a swete fysh but it is a qualy meat and perylous for a mans body. For commonly he gyueth an introduction to the febres. And yf that he be eaten rawe, he may be cause of mannes deth, whiche hath oftentymes bene sene. These be his baytes. In Marche and in Apryll take a fayre freshe chese, and laye it on the borde, and cut it in small square peces of the length of your hooke. Than take a candell and brenne it at the ende at the poynt of the hooke vnto the tyme that it be yelowe, and than bynde it on your hooke with fletchers sylke, and make it tough lyke a welbede, this bayte is good all the sommer season. In May and Iune take the hautorne worme, & the great red worme, & nip of ye head and put vpon your hooke a cod worme before, and that is a good bayte. In Iuly take the read worme for chese, & the hauthorne together, also the water docke lefe worme together in August, and for al the yere, take the talow of a shepe, and soft chese of eche like much, & a lytel hony, & grinde or stampe them together long & temper it till it be tough and put thereto a lytell floure, & make it in small pelletes & that is a good bait to angle w^t at the ground, & loke y^t it sinke in the water, or else it is not good to this purpose.

The Carpe is a deinteous fishe, but there be but few in England, and therefore I wryte least of him he is an euill fyssh to take. For he is so strong enarmed in ye mouthe that there may no weke harneis holde him. And as touchyng his baytes I haue but lytle knowledg of it, and I were lothe to wryte more then I knowe, and haue proued. But well I know that the red worme and the menow ben good baytes for hym, at all tymes, as I haue heard saye of persons credyble, and also found writen in bookes of credence.

The Cheuin is a stately fishe, & his head is a deinty morsell. There is no fish so strongly enarmed w^t scales on the bodye, and because he is a strong byter: he hath the more baytes which ben these. In Marche the red worme at the ground, for commonly then he wil bite there at all tyme of the yere, yf he be any thyng hungry.

In Apryll the dyche Canker that breedeth in the tree, & worme that breedeth betwene the rynde and the tree of an oke. The red worme, and the yong frosshes when the feete be cut of. Also the stone fly, the bob vnder the cow torde, the read snayle. In Maye, the bayte that breedeth in the osyer lefe, and the docke canker together vpon your hooke, and a bayte that breedeth on a ferne lefe, the read worme, and a bayte that breedeth on a hauthorne, and a bayte that breedeth on an oken lefe, and a sylke worme, & a cod worme together. In Iune take the creker and the dorre, and also a read worm, the head cutte of and a cod-worme before, and put them on the hooke. Also a bayte in the osyer lefe, yong frosshes, the thre fete cut of by the body & the .iiii. by the knee. The bayte on the hauthorne, & the codworme together and also a grub that breedeth on a dung hill, a great greshop and the humblebee in the medow. Also young bees, and young hornettes, also a great brendeth flye that breedeth in pathes medowes, and the flye that is amonge pysmer hylles. In August take worte wormes, and magottes to Mychelmas. In September the read worme, and also take the baytes when you may get them, that is to wete, cheryes, and young myce not heared, and the house combe.

The Breme is a noble fyshhe, and a deynteous, and ye shall angle for hym from Marche vnto August with a red worme, and then with a butter flye, and a grene flye, and with a bayte that breedeth among greene reed, and a bayte that breedeth in the barke of a dead tree, and for bremettes take magottes. And from that tyme forth all the yeare after take the read worme, and in the ryuer brownebread. More baytes there be, not easy, and therefore let them passe.

The Tenche is a good fysshe, and healeth al maner of other fish that ben hurt if thei may come to him. He is moste part of the yere in the mud, and styreth moste in Iune and Iuly, and in other season but lytle. He is an euyll byter, and his baytes bene these for all the yeare, browne bread tosted with hony, in lykenes of a buttred lofe, and the great read worme. And take the blacke bloud in the harte of a shepe, and floure & hony, and tempre them altogether, somedele softer then past, and anoynt the read worme there with, bothe for this fyshhe and for other. And they wyll byte muche the better thereat, at all tymes.

The Perche is a deynteous fysshe, and passing holsome and after byting. These ben his baytes. In Marche the red worme. In Apryll the bobbe vnder the cow torde. In May the Hothorne worme, & the cod worme. In Iune the bayte that breedeth in an olde fallen oke, and the great canker. In Iuly the bayte that bredeth on the oyser lefe & the bob that bredeth on a dunghyll, & the hathorne worme & the codworme. In August the read worme & magottes, and all the yeare after take read worme for the best.

The Roche is an easy fyshhe to take, & if he be fat & penned then is he good meat & these ben his baytes. In Marche the read worme. In Apryll the bobbe vnder the cowe torde. In may the bayte that breedeth on the oke lefe, and the bob on the dunghyll. In Iune the bayte that bredeth on oysyer & the codworm. In Iuly house spyes & the bait that bredeth on an oke & the nut worme, & mathewes, and maggots vnto Mychelmas, & then after y^t the fat of bakon.

The Dace is a gentyl fyche to take & if it be wel refert then it is good meate. In March his bayte is a redworm. And in Apryll the bob vnder the cowtorde. In Maye the docke canker, & the bayte on the .othorne and on the oke lefe. In Iune the codworme & the bayte on the oyser, and the whyte grub in the dunghill. In Iuly take house spies & flyes y^t breede in pismire hilles, the codworme & magots, vnto mychelmas, & if the water be clere, ye shall take fysshe when other take none, & from y^t time forth do as ye do for ye roach, for commonly it is sene y^t their biting & baytes be lyke.

The Bleke is but a feble fysshe, yet he is holsom, his baytes from marche to michelmas be the same y^t I haue writen before for the roche & the darse, sauing all y^t somer season y^t ye may angle for him with a house flie, & in winter season w^t bakon & other baite made as ye hereafter may know

The Ruf is a ryght and holsom fysshe, & ye shall angle to hym with the same baytes in a ll seasons of the yeare & in the same wyse as I haue told you of the perche, for they be lyke in fysshe and in feding, sauyng the ruf is lesse and therefore ye must haue the smaller bayte.

The Flounder is an holsome fysshe & a fre, & a subtyll byter in his maner. For commonly when he souketh his meate he fedeth at the ground, & therfore ye must angle to hym with a ground lyne lyeng, & he hath but one maner of bayte, & that is a red worme, & that moste chefe for all maner of fysshe.

The Gugyn is a good fysshe of the mochenes, and he byteth well at the ground, and his baytes for all the yere ben these, the read worme, codworm & magottes & ye must angle to him w^t a flote, and let youre bayte be nere the botome or els vpon the grounde.

The Menow when he shineth in the water, then he is bitter, and though his body be but littel yet he is a rauenous byter and egre, and ye shall angle for him with the same baytes y^t ye do for the gogon sauing they must be small.

The Eele is a quaisy fysshe, a rauenous & deuourer of the broode of fysshe, & the pyke also is a devourer of fish. I put them both behynde al other for to angle, for this ele ye shall find an whole in ye groun of water, & it is blew & blackish, there put in your hoke till it be a fote within the hole & your bayte shal be a great angle with a menow. The pyke is a good fisshe but for he deuoureth so many as wel of his owne kynde as of other, I loue him the lesse & for to take him ye shal do thus. Take a roche or a fresh hering, & a wyre with a hoke in the ende & put it in at the mouth, & on by the taile down by the ridge of the fresh herying, & than put your lyne of your hoke in after, and draw the hoke into the cheke of the fresh hering, than put a plumbe of lead vpon your lyne a yerde long from your hooke and a flote in mydway betwene, and cast it in a pyt where the pyke vse, and this is the best and moste surest craft to take the pyke. And three maner of taking him there is. Take a frosshe & put it on your hoke at the necke betweene the skin and the body, on the back half, & put on a flote a yerd there in, and cast it where the pike haunteth, & ye shall haue hym.

Another maner, take the same bayte & put it in assafet-ida, & cast it into the water with a corde, and a corke, and ye shall not fayle of hym. And if ye lest to haue a good sport than tye the corde to a goose fote and ye shall se good halyng whether the goose or the pyke shall haue the better.

Nowe ye wote with what baytes and how ye shall angle vnto euery maner of fisshe. Now I wil tel you how ye shall keepe and feede your quicke baytes, ye shall feede and keepe them all in generall, but euery maner by hym selfe with such things in and on which they brede. And as long as they be quicke & new they be fine. But when they haue bene in a sloughe or els dead than bene they nought. Out of these bene excepted three broodes, that is to wyte of Hornettes, Humblebees, and Waspes, Whoome ye shall bake in breade, and after dyppe their headdes in bloude and lette them drye. Also excepte magottes, whyche whan they be breed greate with their naturall feedyng, ye shall feede them forthermore with shepes talowe & wyth a cake made of floure & hony. thenne woll they be more grete. And whan you haue clensyd theym wyth sonde in a bagge of blanket kepte hote vnder your gowne or other warmm thyng two houres or thre, thenn ben they beste & redy to angle wyth. And of the frosshe kytte the legge by the knee. of the grasshop the leggys & wynges by the body.

Thyse ben baytes made to laste all the yere. Fyrste been floure & lene flesh of the hepis of a cony or of a catte: virgyn wexe & shepys tallowe: and braye theym in a mortar: And thene tempre it at the fyre wyth a lytell puryfyed hony: & soo make it vp in lytyll ballys & bayte therwyth your hokys after theyr quan-tyte. & this is a good bayte for all manere fresshe fysshe.

Another, take the sewet of a shepe & cheese in lyke quantyte: & braye theim togider long in a mortere: And take thenne floure & tempre it therwyth. and after that alaye it wyth hony & make ballys therof. and that is for the barbell in especyall.

Another for darse, & roche & bleke. Take whete & sethe it well & thenne put it in blood all a daye & a nyghte, and it is a good bayte.

For baytes for grete fyssh kepe specyally this rule. Whan ye haue take a grete fysshe: vndo the mawe. & what ye fynde therin make that your bayte: for it is beste.

Thyse ben the .xij. flyes wyth whyche ye shall angle to ye trought and grayllyng and dubbe lyke as ye shall now here me tell.

The donne flye the body of the donne woll & the wyngis of the pertryche. A nother doone flye. the body of blacke woll: the wynges of the blackyst drake: and the Iay vnder the wynges & vnder the tayle.

Apryll.

The stone flye. the body of blacke wull: & yelowe vnder the wynge. and vnder the tayle & the wynges of the drake. In the begynnynge of May a good flye. the body of roddyd wull and lappid abowte wyth blacke sylke: the wynges of the drake & of the redde capons hakyll.

May.

The yelow flye. The body of yelow wull: the wynges of the redde cocke hakyll & of the drake lyttyd yelow. The blacke louper. the body of blacke wull & lappyd abowte wyth the herle of the pecok tayle: & the wynges of the redde capon w[t] a blewe heed.

Iune.

The donne cutte: the body of blacke wull & a yelow lyste after eyther syde: the wynges of the bosarde bounde on wyth barkyd hempe. The maure flye. the body of doske wull the wynges of the blackest mayle of the wylde drake. The tandy flye at saynt Wyllyams daye. the body of tandy & wull & the wynges contrary eyther ayenst other of the whitest mayle ofthe wylde drake.

Iuly.

The waspe flye. The body of blacke wull & lappid abowte w[t] yelow threde: the winges of the bosarde. The shell flye at saynt Thomas daye. the body of grene wull & lappyd abowt wyth the herle of the pecoks tayle: wynges of the bosarde.

August.

The drake flye. the body of blacke wull & lappyd abowte wyth blacke sylke: wynges of the mayle of the blacke drake wyth a blacke heed,

Thyse fygures are put here in ensample of your hokes.

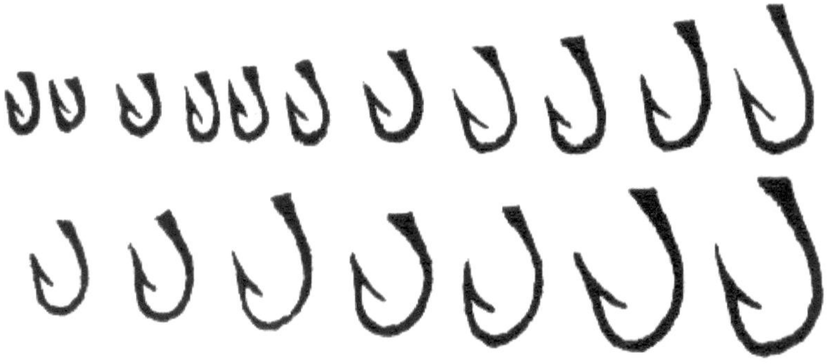

Here folowyth the order made to all those whiche shall haue the vnderstondynge of this forsayde treatyse & vse it for theyr pleasures.

Ye that can angle & take fysshe to your plesures as this forsayd treatyse techyth & shewyth you: I charge & requyre you in the name of alle noble men that ye fysshe not in noo poore mannes seuerall water: as his ponde: stewe: or other necessary thynges to kepe fysshe in wythout his lycence & good wyll.

Nor that ye vse not to breke noo mannys gynnys lyenge in their weares & in other places due vnto theym. Ne to take the fysshe awaye that is taken in theym. For after a fysshe is taken in a mannys gynne yfthe gynne be layed in the comyn waters: or elles in suche waters as he hireth it is his owne propre goodes. And yf ye take it awaye ye robbe hym: whyche is a ryght shamfull dede to ony noble man to do that that the uys & brybours done: whyche are punysshed for theyr euyll dedes by the necke & otherwyse whan they maye be aspyred & taken. And also yf ye doo in lyke manere as this treatise sheweth you: ye shall haue no nede to take of other mennys: whiles ye shal haue enough of your owne takyng yf ye lyste to labour therfore, whyche shall be to you a very pleasure to se the fayr bryght shynynge scalyd fysshes dyceyued by your crafty meanes and drawen vpon londe.

Also that you breke no mannys hegges in goyng about your disportes.

And take good hede that in goyng about your disportes ye open no mans gates but that ye shyt them agayn. Also ye shal not vse this for said crafty disortes for no couetousnes, to the encreasing & sparing of your mony onely, but pryncypally for your solace, & to cause the helth of your body, & specially of your soule. For when you purpose to go on your disportes in fysshing, ye wyll not desyre greatlye many persons with you which might let you of your game. And then ye may serve God deuotedly in saying effectually your customable prayers. And thus doyng: ye shall eschewe and also auoyde many vyces, as ydelnes whiche is pryncypall cause to enduce man to many other vices as it is ryght well knowen. Also ye shall not be to rauenous in takyng of your sayde game, as too muche at one tyme whiche ye may lightly doo yf ye do in euery poynt as this present treatyse shewed you, whiche should lyghtly be the occasion to destroye your owne disportes and other mens also. And when ye haue a sufficient messe, ye should couet no more at that tyme, Also ye shal helpe your selfe to nouryshe the game in all that ye may and also to destroye all suche thynges as bene deuourers of it.

Finis.

And all those that dooth after this rule shall haue the blessyng of God and Saynt Peter, whiche he them graunt that with his precious bloud vs bought. Amen.

Here endeth the booke of Haukyng huntyng, and fysshyng, with other dyvers matters.

TREATISE OF FISHING WITH AN ANGLE

(Modern English)

HERE BEGINS THE TREATISE OF FISHING WITH AN ANGLE

Solomon in his proverbs says that a good spirit makes a flowering age, that is, a happy age and a long one. And since it is true, I ask this question, 'Which are the means and the causes that lead a man into a happy spirit?" Truly, in my best judgement, it seems that they are good sports and honest games which a man enjoys without any repentance afterward. Thence it follows that good sports and honest games are the cause of a man's happy old age and long life. And therefore, I will now choose among four good sports and honest games: to wit, of hunting, hawking, fishing, and fowling. The best, in my simple opinion, is fishing, called angling, with a rod and a line and a hook. And of that I will talk as my simple mind will permit: not only because of the reasoning of Solomon, but also for the assertion that medical science makes in this manner:

Si tibi deficiant medici, medici tibi fiant

Haec tria-mens laeta, labor, et moderatadiaeta.

You shall understand that this means, if a man lacks leech or medicine, he shall make three things his leech and medicine, and he will never need any more. The first of them is a happy mind. The second is work which isn't too onerous. The third is a good diet, First, if a man wishes ever more to have merry thoughts and be happy, he must avoid all quarrelsome company and all places of debate, where he might have any causes to be upset. And if he wishes to have a job which is not too hard, he must then organise, for his relaxation and pleasure, without care, anxiety, or trouble, a cheerful occupation which gives him good heart and in which will raise his spirits. And if he wishes to have a moderate diet, he must avoid all places of revelry, which is the cause of overindulgence and sickness. And he must withdraw himself to places of sweet and hungry air, and eat nourishing and digestible meats.

Now then, I will describe these sports or games to establish, as well as I can, which is the best of them; although the right noble and very worthy prince, the Duke of York, lately called the Master of Game, has described the pleasures of hunting, just as I would describe it and all the others. For hunting, to my way of thinking, is too laborious. The hunter must always run and follow his hounds, exercising and sweating heavily. He blows on his horn till his lips blister; and when he thinks he is chasing a hare, very often it is a hedgehog. Thus he hunts and knows not what he is after. He comes home in the evening soaking through, scratched, his clothes torn, his feet wet, covered in mud. This hound lost and that one crippled. Such upsets and many others happen to the hunter which, for fear of the displeasure of the hunters, I dare not discuss. Thus, in truth, it seems to me that this is not the best sport or game of the four mentioned.

The sport of hawking is hard work and difficult too, it seems to me. For the falconer often loses his hawks, as the hunter his hounds Then his game and pleasure is gone. Very often he shouts and whistles till he has a raging thirst. His hawk flies to a branch and ignores him. When he would have her fly at game, then she wants a bath. With poor feeding she will get the frounce, the ray, the cray, and many other illnesses that cause them to die. This proves that this is not the best sport and game of the four discussed.

The sport and game of fowling seems to me the worst. For in winter season the fowler has no luck except in the hardest and coldest weather, which is burdensome. When he would go to his traps, he cannot because of the cold. He makes many traps and snares, yet he fares badly. In the morning, the dew soaks him up to his thighs. I could say more, but will leave off for fear of upset.

Thus, it seems to me that hunting and hawking and also fowling are so tiresome and unpleasant that none of them can succeed nor can they be the best way of bringing a man into a happy frame of mind, which is the cause of long life according to the said proverb of Solomon. Doubtless then, it follows that the winner should be the sport of fishing with a hook. For every other kind of fishing is also tiresome and unpleasant, often making folks very wet and cold, which many times has been the cause of great illness. But the angler will not suffer cold nor discomfort nor anger, unless he be the cause himself. For he can lose at the most only a line or a hook, of which he can have plenty of his own making, as this simple treatise will teach him. So then his loss is not serious, and nothing else can upset him, except that some fish may break away after he has been hooked, or else he may catch nothing: these are not serious. For if the angler fails with one, he may not fail with another, if he does as this treatise teaches: unless there are no fish in the water. And yet, at the very least, he has his wholesome and pleasant walk at his ease, and a sweet breath of the fragrant smell of the meadow flowers, to make him hungry. He hears the melodious harmony of birds. He sees the young swans, herons, ducks, coots, and many other birds with their broods, which to me seems better than all the noise of hounds, the blasts of horns, and the clamour of birds that hunters, falconers, and fowlers can produce. And if the angler catches fish, surely then there is no happier man. Also whoever wishes to practice the sport of angling, he must rise early, which thing is profitable to a man in this way. That is, to wit: most for the welfare of his soul. For it will cause him to be holy, and for the health of his body. For it will cause him to be well, also for the increase of his goods, for it will make him rich. As the old English proverb says: "Whoever will rise early shall be holy, healthy, and happy."

Thus have I proved, as I intended, that the sport and game of angling is the best means and cause that brings a man into a merry spirit, which according to the said proverb of Solomon and the said teaching of medicine makes a flowering age and a long one. And therefore, to all you that are virtuous, gentle, and freeborn, I write and make this simple treatise which follows, by which you may have the full craft of angling to amuse you as you please, in order that your life may be more successful and last longer.

If you want to be crafty in angling, you must first learn to make your tackle, that is, your rod, your lines of different colours. After that, you must know how you should angle, in what place of the water, how deep, and what time of day. For what manner of fish, in what weather; how many impediments there are in the fishing that is called angling. And especially with what baits for each different fish in each month of the year. How you shall make your baits breed. Where you will find the baits: and how you will keep them. And for the most crafty thing, how you are to make your hooks of steel and of iron. Some for the artificial fly: and some for the float and the ground-line, as you will hear afterward all these things talked about openly so that you may learn.

And how you should make your rod skilfully, here I shall teach you. You must cut, between Michaelmas and Candlemas, a fair staff of a fathom and a half long and as thick as your arm, of hazel, willow, or ash. And soak it in a hot oven, and set it straight. Then let it cool and dry for a month. Take them and tie it tight with a cockshoot cord, and bind it to a form or a perfectly square, large piece of timber. Then take a plumb wire that is smooth and straight and sharp at one end. And heat the sharp end in a charcoal fire till it is white-hot: and then burn the staff through with it: always straight in the pith at both ends, till they meet. And after that, burn it in the lower end with a spit for roasting birds, and with other spits, each bigger than the last, and always the largest last: so that you make your hole taper. Then let it lie still and cool for two days. Untie it then and let it dry in a house-roof in the smoke until it is thoroughly dry. In the same season, take a good rod of green hazel, and soak it even and straight and let it dry with the staff. And when they are dry, make the rod fit the hole in the staff, into half the length of the staff. And to make the other half of the top section, take a fair shoot of blackthorn, crabtree, medlar, or juniper, cut in the same season: and well soaked and straight. And bind them together neatly so that the top section may go exactly all the way into the said hole. Then shave your staff down and make it taper. Then bind the staff at both ends with long hoops of iron or fasten in the neatest manner, with a spike in the lower end fastened with a catch so that you can take your top section in and out. Then set your upper section a handbreadth inside the other end of your staff in such a way that the thickness of the sections matches. Bind your top section at the other end as far down as the joint with a cord of six hairs. Fix the cord and tie it firmly at the top, with a loop to fasten on your fishing line. And so you will make yourself a rod so secret that you can walk with it, and no one will know what you are doing. It will be light and well balanced to fish with as you wish.

And for your greater convenience, here is a picture of it as an example:

After you have made your rod, you must learn to colour your lines of hair this way. First, you must take, from the tail of a white horse, the longest and best hairs that you can find; and the rounder it is, the better it is. Divide it into six bunches, and you shall colour every part by itself in a different colour. As yellow, green, brown, tawny, russet, and dusky colours.

And to make a good green colour on your hair, you shall do thus. Take a quart of small ale and put it in a little pan, and add to it half a pound of alum. And put your hair in it, and let it boil softly half an hour. Then take out your hair and let it dry. Then take a half-gallon of water and put it in a pan. And put in it two handfuls of a yellow dye, and press it with a tile-stone, and let it boil gently half an hour. And when it is yellow on the scum, put in your hair with half a pound copperas, beaten to powder, and let it boil gently half an hour. And then set it down and let it cool five or six hours. Then take out the hair and dry it. And it is then the finest green there is for the water, And the more copperas you add to it, the better it is. Or else instead, use verdigris.

Another way, you can make a brighter green, thus. Woad your hair in a woad vat until it is a light blue-grey colour. And then boil it in yellow vegetable dye as I have described, except that you must not add to it either copperas or verdigris.

To make your hair yellow, prepare it with alum as I have explained already. And after that with yellow vegetable dye without copperas or verdigris.

Another yellow you shall make thus. Take a half a gallon of small ale, and crush three handfuls of walnut leaves, and put them together. And put in your hair until it is as deep a yellow as you will have it.

To make russet hair, take of strong lye a pint and a half and half a pound of soot and a little juice of walnut leaves and a quarter of a pound of alum; and put them all together in a pan and boil them well. And when it is cold, put in your hair till it is as dark as you will have it.

To make a brown colour, take a pound of soot and a quart of ale, and boil it with as many walnut leaves as you wish. And when they turn black, take it off the fire. And put your hair in it, and let it lie still till it is as brown as you will have it.

To make another brown, take strong ale and soot and blend them together, and put therein your hair for two days and two nights, and it will be a right good colour.

To make a tawny colour, take lime and water, and put them together; and also put your hair therein four or five hours. Then take it out and put it in tanner's ooze a day, and it will be as fine a tawny colour as we need for our purpose.

The sixth part of your hair, you must keep still white for lines for the dubbed hook, to fish for the trout and grayling, and for small lines to use for the roach and the dace.

When your hair is thus coloured, you must know for which waters and for which seasons they should be used. The green colour in all clear water from April till September. The yellow colour in every clear water from September till November: for it is like the weeds and other types of grass which grow in the waters and rivers, when they are broken. The russet colour serves all the winter until the end of April, as well in rivers as in pools or lakes. The brown colour serves for that water that is black, sluggish, in rivers or in other waters. The tawny colour for those waters that are heathy or marshy.

Now you must make your lines in this way. First, see that you have an instrument like the one shown in the following picture. Then take your hair and cut off from the small end a large handful or more, for it is neither strong nor yet sure. Then turn the top to the tail each in equal amount, and divide it into three parts. Then plait each part at the one end by itself. And at the other end plait all three together: and put this same end in the other end of your instrument, the end that has but one cleft. And make the other end tight with the wedge four fingers from the end of your hair. Then twist each strand the same way and pull it tight: and fasten them in the three clefts equally well. Then take out that other end and twist it whichever way it goes best. Then stretch it a little and plait it so that it will not come undone: and that is good. And to know how to make your instrument, see, here it is in a picture. And it shall be made of wood, except the bolt underneath; which must be of iron.

When you have as many of the lengths as you suppose will suffice for the length of a line, then you must tie them together with a water knot or else a duchess knot. And when your knot is tied, cut off the unused ends a straw's breadth from the knot. Thus you will make your lines fair and fine, and also completely secure for any type of fish. .

You shall understand that the subtlest and hardest art in making your tackle is to make your hooks. For the making of which you must have suitable files, thin and sharp and beaten small; a semi-clamp of iron: a bender: a pair of long and small tongs: a hard knife, somewhat thick: an anvil: and a little hammer. And for small fish you shall make your hooks in this manner, of the smallest square needles of steel that you can find. You shall put the square needle in a red charcoal fire till it is of the same colour as the fire. Then take it out and let it cool, and you will find it well tempered for filing. Then raise the barb with your knife and make the point sharp. Then temper it again, for otherwise it will break in the bending. Then bend it like the bend shown here as an example. And you shall make greater hooks in the same way out of larger needles: such as embroiderers' or tailors' or shoemakers' needles. Spear points or shoemakers' needles especially are the best hooks for great fish. And [see that they bend] at the point when they are tested; otherwise they are not good. When the hook is bent, beat the hinder end out broad, and file it smooth to prevent fraying of your line. Then put it in the fire again and give it an easy red heat. Then suddenly quench it in water, and it will be hard and strong. And for you to have knowledge of your instruments, see them here in portrayed in the picture.

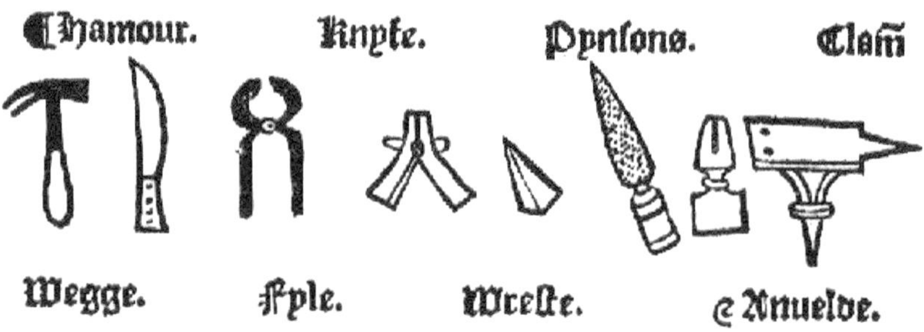

When you have made your hooks as you have been taught, then you must attach them on your lines, according to size and strength in this manner. You must take fine red silk, and if it is for a large hook, then double it, don't twist it. Otherwise, for small hooks, let it be single: and with it, thickly bind the line there for a straw's breadth from the end of the hook where your line is placed. Then set your hook there, and wrap it with the same thread for two-thirds of the length that is to be wrapped. And when you come to the third part, turn the end of your line back upon the wrapping, double, and wrap it thus double for the third part. Then put your thread in at the loop twice or thrice, and let it go each time round about the shank of your hook. Then wet the loop and pull it until it is tight. And be sure that your line always lies inside your hooks and not outside. Then cut off the end of the line and the thread as close as you can without cutting the knot.

Now that you know how big a hook to angle with for every fish, I will tell you with how many hairs you must angle for every kind of fish. For the minnow, with a line of one hair. For the growing roach, the bleak, the gudgeon, and the ruffee, with a line of two hairs. For the dace and the great roach, with a line of three hairs. For the perch, the flounder, and small bream, with four hairs. For the chevin-chub, the bream, the tench, and the eel, with six hairs. For the trout, grayling, barbel, and the great chub, with nine hairs. For the great trout, with twelve hairs. For the salmon, with fifteen hairs. And for the pike, with a chalk line made brown with your brown colouring as described earlier, strengthened with a wire, as you will hear hereafter when I speak of the pike.

Your lines must be weighted with lead, and you must know that the nearest sinker to the hook should be a full foot and more separated from it, and every sinker of a weight suitable for the thickness of the line. There are three kinds of sinkers for a running ground-line. And for the float set upon the stationary ground-line ten weights all joining together. On the running ground-line, nine or ten small ones. The float sinker must be so heavy that the least pluck of any fish can pull it down into the water. And make your weights round and smooth so that they do not stick on stones or on weeds. And for the better understanding see them here in picture.

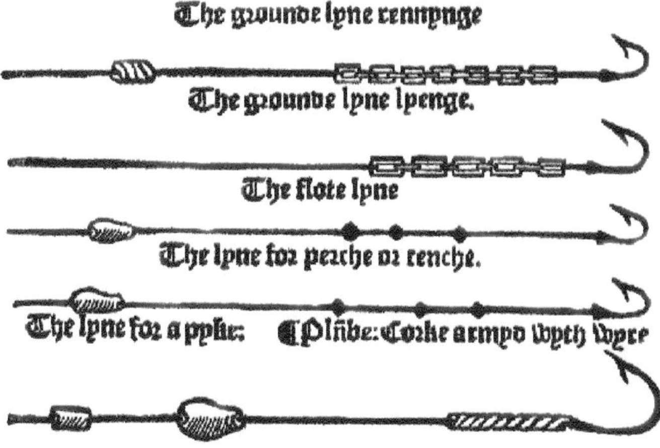

Then you are to make your floats in this manner. Take a good cork that is clean without any holes, and bore it through with a small hot iron: and put a quill in it even and straight. The larger the float, the larger the quill and the larger the hole. Then shape it large in the middle and small at both ends, and especially sharp in the lower end, and similar to the pictures which follow. And make them smooth on a grinding stone, or on a tile stone. And see that the float for one hair is no more than pea-sized; for two hairs; as a bean; for twelve hairs, as a walnut. And so every line according to proportion. All kinds of lines that are not for the ground must have floats, and the running ground-line must have a float. The stationary ground-line doesn't need a float.

Now I have taught you to make all your tackle. Here I will tell you how you shall angle. You will fish: understand that there are six ways of angling. The first is at the bottom for the trout and other fish. Another is at the bottom at an arch or at a pool, where it ebbs and flows, for bleak, roach, and dace. The third is with a float for all manner of fish. The fourth, with a minnow for the trout without lead or float. The fifth is running in the same way for roach and dace with one or two hairs and a fly. The sixth is with an artificial fly for the trout and grayling. And for the first and principal point in angling, always keep away from the water, from the sight of the fish: either keep back on the land or else behind a bush, so that the fish can't see you. For if they do, they will not bite. Also take care that your shadow does not fall on the water any more than it might, for that is a thing which will soon frighten the fish. And if a fish is frightened, he will not bite for a long time after. For all kinds of fish that feed at the bottom, you must angle for them at the bottom, so that your hooks will run or lie on the bottom. And for all other fish that feed above, you must angle for them in the middle of the water, or somewhat beneath or somewhat above. For the bigger the fish, the nearer he lies to the bottom of the water; and the smaller the fish, the more he swims above. The third good point is when the fish bites, that you be not too quick to strike, nor too slow. For you must wait till you suppose that the bait is fairly in the mouth of the fish, and then wait no longer. And this is for the bottom. And for the float, when you see it pulled softly under the water or else carried softly upon the water, then strike. And see that you never strike too hard for the strength of your line, for fear of breaking it. And if you have the fortune to hook a great fish with a small tackle, then you must lead him in the water and labour with him there until he is drowned and overcome. Then take him as well as you can or may, and always beware that you do not pull beyond the strength of your line. And as much as you can, do not let him come out of the end of your line straight from you, but keep him ever under the rod and always hold him there, so that your line can sustain and bear his leaps and his plunges with the help of your rod and of your hand.

Here I will declare to you in what place of the water you must angle. You should angle in a pool or in standing water in every place where it is at all deep. There is not a great choice of places where a pool is of any depth. For it is but a prison for fish, and they live for the most part in hunger like prisoners; and therefore it takes the less art to catch them. But in a river, you shall angle in every place where it is deep and clear by the bottom: for example gravel or clay without. mud or weeds. And especially if there an eddy or a cover. For example a hollow bank: or big roots of trees: or long weeds floating above in the water where the fish can cover and hide themselves at certain times when they like. Also it is good to angle in deep, swift streams, and also in waterfalls and weirs: and in floodgates and mill-races. And it is good to angle where the water rests by the bank: and where the current runs close by: and it is deep and clear at the bottom: and in any other places where you can see any fish rise or feeding.

Now you must know what time of the day you should angle. From the beginning of May until it is September, the biting time is early in the morning from four o'clock until eight o'clock. And in the afternoon, from four o'clock until eight o'clock, but not so good as in the morning. And if there is a cold, whistling wind and a dark, lowering day. For a dark day is much better to angle in than a clear day. From the beginning of September until the end of April, don't ignore any time of the day. Also many pool fishes will bite best at noontime. And if at any time of the day you see the trout or grayling leap, angle for him with an artificial fly appropriate to that same month. And where the water ebbs and flows, the fish will bite in some place at the ebb, and in some place at the flood. After that, they will rest behind stakes and arches of bridges and other places of that sort.

Here you should know in what weather you must angle: as I said before, in a dark, lowering day when the wind blows softly. And in summer season when it is burning hot, then it is no good. From September until April on a fair, sunny day, it is right good to angle. And if the wind in that season comes from any part of the east: the weather then is no good. And when it snows or hails, or there is a great tempest, with thunder or lightning, or sweltering hot weather, then it is no good for angling.

Now you must know that there are twelve kinds of impediments which cause a man to take no fish, without other common causes that may happen by chance. The first is if your tackle is not adequate nor suitably made. The second is if your baits are not good or fine. The third is if you do not angle in biting time. The fourth is if the fish are frightened by the sight of a man. The fifth, if the water is very thick: white or red from any recent flood. The sixth, if the fish cannot stir because of the cold. The seventh, if the weather is hot. The eighth, if it rains. The ninth, if it hails or snow falls. The tenth is if there is a tempest. The eleventh is if there is a great wind The twelfth if the wind is in the east, and that is worst, for commonly, both winter and summer, the fish will not bite then. The west and north winds are good, but the south is best.

And now that I have told you, in all points, how to make your tackle and how you must fish with it, it makes sense that you should know with what baits you must angle for every kind of fish in every month of the year, which is the effect of the art. And without these baits being well known by you, all your other skills taught until now will not be of much use. For you cannot bring a hook into a fish's mouth without a bait. Baits for every kind of fish and for every month follow here in this way.

Because the salmon is the most stately fish that any one can angle for in fresh water. Therefore I intend to begin with him. The salmon is a noble fish, but he is difficult to catch. For commonly he lies only in deep places of great rivers. And for the most part he keeps to the middle of the water: that a man cannot come at him. And he is in season from March until Michaelmas. In which season you should angle for him with these baits when you can get them. First, with a red worm in the beginning and end of the season. And also with a grub that grows in a dunghill. And especially with an excellent bait that grows on a water dock. And he doesn't bite at the bottom but at the float. Also you may take him: but it is seldom seen with a dubbed hook at such times as he leaps, in the same style and manner as you catch a trout or a grayling. And these baits are well proven baits for the salmon.

The trout, because he is a right dainty fish and also a right fervent biter, we shall speak of next. He is in season from March until Michaelmas. He is on clean gravel bottom and in a stream. You can angle for him at all times with a lying or running ground-line: except in leaping time and then with a dubbed hook; and early with a running ground-line, and later in the day with a float line. You shall angle for him in March with a minnow hung on your hook by the lower nose, without float or sinker: drawing it up and down in the stream till you feel him take. In the same time, angle for him with a ground-line with an red worm as the most sure. In April, take the same baits, and also the lamprey, otherwise named "seven eyes," also the cankerworm that grows in a great tree, and the red snail. In May take the stone fly and the grub under the cow turd, and the silkworm, and the bait that grows on a fern leaf. In June, take a red worm and nip off the head, and put a codworm on your hook before it. In July, take the great red worm and the codworm together. In August, take a flesh fly and the big red worm and bacon fat, and bind them on your hook. In September, take the red worm and the minnow. In October, take the same, for they are special for the trout at all times of the year. From April to September the trout leaps; then angle for him with dubbed hook appropriate to the month these dubbed hooks you will find at the end of this treatise; and the months with them.

The grayling by another name called umber is a delicious fish to man's month. And you can catch him just as you can the trout. And these are his baits. In March and in April, the red worm. In May, the green worm: a little ringed worm, the dock canker, and the hawthorn worm. In June, the bait that grows between the tree and the bark of an oak. In July, a bait that grows on a fern leaf and the big red worm. And nip off the head and put a codworm on your hook before it. In August, the red worm, and a dock worm. And all the year afterward, a red worm

The barbel is a sweet fish, but it is a queasy food and a dangerous one for man's body. For commonly, he introduces the fevers. And if he is eaten raw, he may be the cause of a man's death: which often has been seen. These are his baits. In March and in April, take fair fresh cheese: lay it on a board and cut it in small square pieces the length of your hook. Then take a candle and burn it on the end at the point of your hook until it is yellow. And then bind it on your hook with arrow maker's silk, and make it rough like a welbede. This bait is good for all the summer season. In May and June, take the hawthorn worm and the big red worm and nip off the head and put a codworm on your hook before them and that is a good bait. In July, take the red worm chiefly and the hawthorn worm together. Also the water-dock leaf worm and the hornet worm together. In August and for all the year, take mutton fat and soft cheese, of each the same amount, and a little honey and grind or beat them together a long time, and work it until it is tough. Add to it a little flour and make it into small pellets. And that is a good bait to angle with at the bottom. And see that it sinks in the water, or else it is not good for this purpose.

The carp is a dainty fish, but there are only a few in England, and therefore I will write the less of him. He is an evil fish to take. For he is so strongly armoured in the mouth that no light tackle may hold him. And as regards his baits, I have but little knowledge of it, and I am reluctant to write more than I know and have tried. But well I know that the red worm and the minnow are good baits for him at all times as I have heard reliable persons tell and also found written in books of credence.

The chubb is a stately fish and his head is a dainty morsel. There is no fish so greatly armoured with scales on the body. And because be is a strong biter he has the more baits, which are these. In March, the red worm at the bottom for commonly he will bite these and at all times of the year if he is at all hungry. In April the ditch canker that grows in the tree. A worm that grows between the bark and the wood of an oak. The red worm: and the young frogs when the feet are cut off. Also, the stone fly, the grub under the cow turd: the red snail. In May, the bait that grows on the osier leaf and the dock canker together on your hook. Also a bait that grows on a fern leaf: the codworm, and a bait that grows on a hawthorn. And a bait that grows on an oak leaf and a silkworm and a codworm together. In June, take the cricket and the dor; and also a red worm: the head cut off and a codworm before it: and put them on the hook. Also a bait on the osier leaf: young frogs with three feet cut off at the body: and the fourth at the knee. The bait on the hawthorn and the codworm together; and a grub that breeds in a dunghill: and a large grasshopper. In July, the grasshopper and the bumblebee on the meadow. Also young bees and young hornets. Also a great, brindled fly that grows in paths of meadows, and the fly that is among anthills. In August, take caterpillars and maggots until Michaelmas. In September, the red worm: and also take these baits when you can get them: that is to say: cherries: young mice without hair: and the honeycomb.

The bream is a noble fish and a dainty one. And you shall angle for him from March until August with an red worm: and then with a butterfly and a green fly. And with a bait that grows among green reeds: and a bait that grows in the bark of a dead tree. And for young bream, take maggots. And from that time forth for all the year afterward, take the red worm: and in the river, brown bread. There are more baits than these, but they are not easy, and I let them pass over.

A tench is a good fish: and heals all sorts of other fish that are hurt if they can come to him. He is the most part of the year in the mud. And he stirs most in June and July: and in other seasons but little. He is a poor biter. His baits are these. For all the year brown bread toasted with honey in the likeness of a buttered loaf: and the great red worm. And for the best bait take the black blood in the heart of a sheep and flour and honey. Work them all together somewhat softer than paste, and anoint there with the red worm: both for this fish and for others. And they will bite much better thereat at all times.

The perch is a dainty fish and passing wholesome, and a free biter. These are his baits. In March, the red worm. In April, the grub under the cow turd. In May, the sloe-thorn worm and the codworm. In June the bait that grows in an old fallen oak, and the green canker. In July, the bait that grows on the osier leaf and the grub that grows on the dunghill: and the hawthorn worm, and the codworm. In August, the red worm and maggots. All the year after, the red worm is best.

The roach is an easy fish to catch. And if he is fat and penned up, then he is good food, and these are his baits. In March, the readiest bait is the red worm. In April, the grub under the cow turd. In May, the bait that grows on the oak leaf and the grub in the dunghill. In June, the bait that grows on the osier and the codworm. In July, houseflies and the bait that grows on all oak; and the nutworm and mathewes and maggots till Michaelmas. And after that, the fat of bacon.

The dace is a noble fish to take, and if it be well fattened, then he is good eating. In March, the best bait is an red worm. In April, the grub under the cow turd. In May the dock canker and the bait on the sloe thorn and on the oak leaf. In June, the codworm and the bait on the osier and the white grub in the dunghill. In July take houseflies, and flies that grow in anthills: the codworm and maggots until Michaelmas. And if the water is clear, you shall catch fish when others take none. And from that time forth, do as you do for the roach. For commonly in their biting and their baits they are alike.

The bleak is but a feeble fish, yet he is wholesome. His baits from March to Michaelmas are the same as I have written before for the roach and dace, except that, all the summer season, as much as you may angle for him with a housefly: and, in the winter season, with bacon and other bait made as you will know after.

The ruffe is a right wholesome fish. And you shall angle to him with the same baits in all seasons of the year in the same way as I have told you of the perch: for they are alike in fishing and feeding except that the ruffe is smaller. And therefore he must have the smaller bait.

The flounder is a noble fish and a free and subtle biter in his manner: For usually, when he sucks in his food, he feeds at the bottom, and therefore you must angle for him with a lying ground-line. And he has but one manner of bait, and that is a red worm, which is the best bait for all kinds of fish.

The gudgeon is a good fish for his size, and he bites well at the bottom. And his baits for all the year are these: the red worm: codworm: and maggots And you must angle for him with a float, and let your bait be near the bottom or else on the bottom.

The minnow, when he shines in the water, then be is better. And though his body is little yet he is a ravenous biter and eager. And you shall angle to him with the same baits that you do for gudgeon: saving that they must be small.

The eel is a queasy fish, a glutton, and a devourer of the young fry of fish. And as the pike also is a devourer of fish I put them both behind all others for angling. For this eel, you must find a hole in the bottom of the water, and it is blue-blackish. There put in your hook till it be a foot within the hole, and your bait should be a great angle worm or a minnow.

The pike is a good fish, but because he devours so many of his own kind as of others, I love him the less. And to catch him, you shall do thus. Take a codling hook: and take a roach or a fresh herring and a wire with a loop in the end: and put it in at the mouth and out at the tail down by the back of the fresh herring. And then put the line of your hook in after, and draw the hook into the cheek of the fresh herring. Then put a lead weight on your line a yard away from your book, and a float midway between; and cast it in a hole where the pike lie. And this is the best and surest way for catching the pike. Another manner of taking him is this. Take a frog and put it on your hook between the skin and the body on the back half, and put on a float a yard away, and cast it where the pike lies, and you shall have him. Another way. Take the same bait and put it in asafetida and cast it in the water with a cord and a cork, and you shall not fail to get him. And if you wish to have a good sport: then tie the cord to a goose's foot, and you will see a good tussle to decide whether the goose or the pike will have the better of it.

Now you know with what baits and how you shall angle to every kind of fish. Now I will tell you how you shall keep and feed your live baits. You shall feed and keep them all together, but each kind by itself with such things in and on which they breed. And as long as they are alive and fresh, they are fine. But when they are sloughing their skin or else dead they are nothing. Out of these are excepted three kinds: That is, to wit of hornets, bumblebees, and wasps. These you must bake in bread, and after dip their heads in blood and let them dry. Also except maggots: which, when they are grown large with their natural feeding, you must feed further with mutton fat and with a cake made of flour and honey; then they will become larger. And when you have cleansed them with sand in a bag of blanket, kept hot under your gown or other warm thing for two hours or three, then they are best and ready to angle with. And of the frog cut off the leg at the knee, of the grasshopper the legs and wings at the body.

These baits are made to last all the year. The first are flour and lean meat from the thigh of a rabbit or a cat: virgin wax, and sheep's fat: and bray them in a mortar: and then temper it at the fire with a little purified honey: and so make it up into little balls, and bait your hooks with it according to their size. And this is a good bait for all manner of fresh fish.

Another, take the suet of a sheep and cheese in equal amounts: and bray them together for a long while in a mortar. And take then flour and temper it therewith, and after that mix it with honey and make balls of it. And that is especially for the barbel.

Another for dace and roach and bleak: take wheat and seethe it well and then put it in blood for a whole day and a night, and it is a good bait.

For baits for great fish, keep specially this rule: When you have taken a great fish, open up the maw, and whatever you find therein, make that your bait, for it is best.

These are the twelve flies with which you shall angle for the trout and grayling; and dub them like you will now hear me tell:

March

The dun fly the body of dun wool and the wings of the partridge. Another dun fly, the body of black wool; the wings of the blackest drake; and the jay under the wing and under the tail.

April

The stone fly, the body of black wool, and yellow under the wing and under the tail; and the wings, of the drake. In the beginning of May, a good fly, the body of reddened wool and lapped about with black silk; the wings, of the drake and the red capon's hackle.

May

The yellow fly, the body of yellow wool; the wings of red cock hackle and of the drake dyed yellow. The black leaper, the body of black wool and lapped about with the herl of the peacock's tail: and the wings of the red capon with a blue head.

June

The dun cut: the body of black wool, and a yellow stripe after either side; the wings of the buzzard, bound on with barked hemp. The maure fly, the body of dusky wool, the wings of the blackest male of the wild drake. The tandy fly at St. William's Day, the body of tandy wool; and the wings contrary either against the other, of the whitest breast feathers of the wild drake.

July

The wasp fly, the body of black wool and lapped about with yellow thread: the wings of the buzzard. The shell fly at St. Thomas' Day, the body of green wool and lapped about with the herl of the peacock's tail: wings of the buzzard.

August

The drake fly, the body of black wool and lapped about with black silk: wings of the breast feathers of the blackest drake, with a black head.

These figures are put here in example of your hooks:

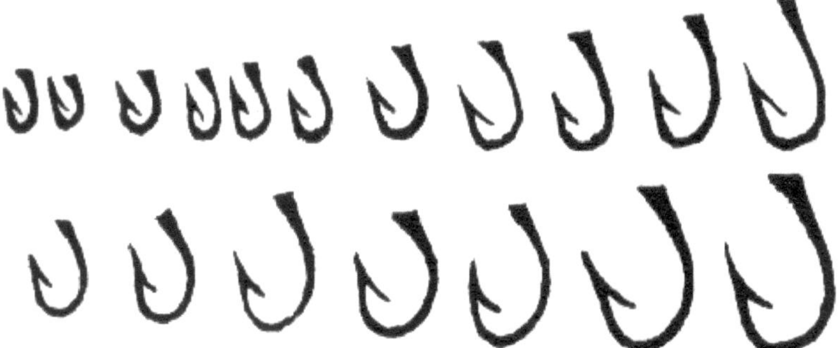

Here follows the order made to all those who shall have the understanding of this aforesaid treatise and use it for their pleasures.

You that can angle and catch fish for your pleasure, as the aforesaid treatise teaches and shows you: I charge and require you in the name of all noble men that you to not fish in any poor man's private water: as his pond: stew: or other necessary things to keep fish in without his license and good will. Nor that you use not to break any man's engines lying in their weirs and in other places due to them. Nor to take the fish away that is taken in them. For after a fish is taken in a man's trap, if the trap is laid in the public waters: or else in such waters as he hires, it is his own personal property. And if you take it away, you rob him: which is a right shameful deed for any gentle man to do, that the thieves and robbers do, who are punished for their evil deeds by the neck and otherwise when they can be found and captured. And also if you do in like manner as this treatise shows you: you will have no need to take other men's fish, while you will have enough of your own catching, if you wish to work for them. It will be a true pleasure to see the fair, bright, shining-scaled fishes deceived by your crafty means and drawn upon the land. Also, I charge you, that you break no man's hedges in going about your sports: nor open any man's gates but that you shut them again. Also, you must not use this aforesaid artful sport for covetousness to increasing or saving of your money only, but principally for your solace and to promote the health of your body and specially of your soul. For when you propose to go on your sports in fishing, you will not desire greatly many persons with you, which might hinder in letting you at your game. And then you can serve God devoutly by earnestly saying your customary prayers. And thus doing, you will eschew and avoid many vices, such as idleness, which is the principal cause to induce man to many other vices, as is right well known. Also, you must not be too greedy in catching your said game as taking too much at one time, which you may easily do if you do in every point as this present treatise shows you in every point. Which could easily be the occasion of destroying your own sport and other men's also. As when you have a sufficient mess you should covet no more as at that time. Also you shall help yourself to nourish the game in all that you may, and to destroy all such things as are devourers of it. And all those that do as this rule shall have the blessing of God and St. Peter. Which he grants them that with his precious blood he bought.

And so that this present treatise should not come into the hands of every idle person who would desire it if it were printed alone by itself and put in a little pamphlet, therefore I have compiled it in a greater volume of diverse books concerning gentle and noble men, to the end that the aforesaid idle persons which should have but little measure in the said sport of fishing should not by this means utterly destroy it

BARKER'S DELIGHT:

OR,

THE ART OF

ANGLING

Wherein are discovered
many rare Secrets
very necessary to be known by all that
delight in that Recreation,
both for catching the Fish,
and dressing thereof.

By *THOMAS BARKER*, an antient
practitioner in the said Art.

Eccles. 3.1.11.

There is a time and season to euery purpose under Heauen: Euery thing is beautifull in his time.

To the
RIGHT HONORABLE
EDWARD *Lord* Montague,
Generall of the Navy, and one of The Lords Commissioners of the Treasury.

NOBLE LORD,

I do present this my book as I have named it *Barker*'s *delight*, to your Honour. I pray God send you safe home to your good Lady and sweet Babes. *Amen, Amen.*

If you shall find any thing delightfull in the reading of it, I shall heartily rejoyce, for I know you are one who takes delight in that pleasure, and have good judgement and experience, as many noble persons & Gentlem. of true piety & honour do & have. The favour that I have found from you, and a great many more that did and do love that pleasure, shall never be bury'd in oblivion by me.

I am now grown old, and am willing to enlarge my little book. I have written no more but my own experience and practise, and have set forth the true ground of Angling, which I have been gathering these threescore yeares, having spent many pounds in the gaining of it, as is well known in the place where I was born and educated, which is *Bracemeale* in the Liberty of *Salop*, being a Freeman and Burgesse of the same City. If any noble or gentle Angler, of what degree soever he be, have a mind to discourse of any of these wayes & experiments, I live in *Henry* the 7th's Gifts, the next doore to the Gatehouse in *Westm.* my name is *Barker*, where I shall be ready, as long as please God, to satisfie them, and maintain my art, during life, which is not like to be long; that the younger fry may have my experiments at a smaller charge than I had them, for, it would be too heavy for every one that loveth that exercise to be at that charge as I was at first in my youth, the losse of my time, with great expenses. Therefore I took it in consideration, and thought fit to let it be understood, & to take pains to set forth the true grounds and wayes that I have found by experience both for fitting of the rods and tackles both for ground-baits and flyes, with directions for the making thereof, with observations for times and seasons, for the ground-baits and flyes, both for day and night, with the dressing, wherein I take as much delight as in the the taking of them, and to shew how I can perform it, to furnish any Lords table, onely with trouts, as it is furnished with flesh, for 16 or 20 dishes. And I have a desire to preserve their health (with help of God) to go dry in their boots and shooes in angling, for age taketh the pleasure from me. My Lord, I am

Your Honours most humble
Servant,

Thomas Barker.

In praise of M. *Barkers* excellent Book of Angling.

CArds, Dice, and Tables pick thy purse;
  Drinking and Drabbing bring a curse.
Hawking and Hunting spend thy chink;
  Bowling and Shooting end in drink.
The fighting-Cock, and the Horse-race
  Will sink a good Estate apace.
Angling doth bodyes exercise.
  And maketh soules holy and wise:
By blessed thoughts and meditation:
  This, this is Anglers recreation!
Health, profit, pleasure, mixt together,
  All sport's to this not worth a feather.

Nagrom Notpoh
Armiger.

Encomium in Authorem,
Thom: Barkerum.

Dulcis Molpomene nectarea carmina fundæ
Ut piscatoris laudes. & gaudia cantem.
Molli perspicio labentia flumina cursu:
Lubrica dulcisono crepitantia murmure saxa;
Atque alto specto ludentes stagmine pisces.
Sprirantem Zephirum, claro tinctumque colore
Coelum: mellifluam musam, volueresq; sonantes.
Dice mihi quæ suavis vita, aut quæ blanda voluptas
Coequare valet piscandi encomia magna?

Ad Lectorem.

Hic liber eximium cursum semitamque docebit
Ambrosea timidos escâ deludere pisces,
Vix faucem poterant hami vitare dolosi:
Artem piscandi generosam expandit amoene,
Amnigenos pisces & arundine vincere longa.
Hic coquus set expers pisces lixare recaptos,
Atque parare suis socius, Convivia rara.

Edmund Swetenham
Gen: Cestriens.

An Encomium on Mr. *Barker*'s exquisite Book of the Art of Angling, *&c.*

I*N Helicon though I could dip my quill,*
To erect my muse and fathom out thy skill:
Alas! too cheap for that which cost so dear;
Great pains, expence and time, full threescore year.
Thou hast unbowell'd brave Dame Natures part
In a Vade mecum, *with Heroick art.*
Thy Booke's a mirrour, there a perfect view
Will still remain, to speak thy praises due.
Perhaps some Rustick currishly will bark
At thee, brave Barker*: but if in the dark*
And silent night thou canst the knave espie,
With the captive Trout he soon shall make a die.
Then rogues thy name wil dread, & from thee gallop
As from the Devil, when 'tis but Tom *of* Salop.
But thou ingenuous spirit, follow him
To christall streames, where nimble fish do swim
With fins display'd, and skipping up the streams:
Then (without help of Phoebus *glorious beams)*
The Trout shall gorge thy bait with pleasure store;
Sweet Philomel *shall eccho on the shore.*
What now remains? thou hast ensnar'd the fish,
And Barkers *Art will make a princely dish.*

Edward Hopton *Gen.*
Hamtoniensis.

Friendly Verses in commenda tion of Mr. Barker's complete work of the Art of Angling.

ORgana piscatorum, ac esca, frequentia piscis,
Tempora piscandi prima, Culina sciens:
Omnia *Barkeri* præbet liber aureus ista.
Artis præceptor cedito, disce, tace.
Discipulos docuit transfigere, ludere lymphæ,
Exhaurire: Petri demito rete, beas.

Thus Englished.

Tackle, Baits, Fish-haunts, skilfull Cookery,
Best times to fish, these Barker *doth descry.*
To strike, play, land thy prize, he tells thee how;
Art angling teachers all to him must bow.
Keep thee but from S. Peters *net, and then*
Blest be thy soul for aye, Amen, Amen.

John Perch
Armig.

Pleasant Hexameter Verses in praise of Mr. Barkers Book of Angling.

TRout, Carp, Perch, Pike, Roch, Dace, Eele, Tench, Bleke,
Gudgeon, Barbell,
Thy truth, experience, love, care, cost, skill, doth describe well.
Valiant, just, honest, true-hearted, *ShrewsburyBarker*,
The Art of Angling discovereth, hitherto darker
Than either Fowling, Hawking, or hunting the swift Hare,
Markam, *Ward*, *Lawson*, dare you with *Barker* now compare?
Of Trouts and huge Pikes you teach us to catch a good dish;
He to make tackle, to kill, and cook also all fish.
All we good Brethren of the Angle do give you your due praise;
But on old *Tom*'s head we mean to put the crown of Baies.

John Hockenhull

Armig. Cestriensis.

On the choyce Treatise called Barker's Delight.

COme come, ye bunglers, learn the skill
The greedy nimble trout to kill.
For twelve pence (now) thou maist learn more
Than in an age was known before;
All baits to know, tackle to fit,
Brave *Barker* I commend thy wit.
What, catch they Prey, and cook the Fish?
And more than this, Sir, can you wish?
Radulphus Hoptonus
Gen. Wigorniens.

In Barkeri librum de arte piscandi Encomium.

BArkeri *in laudem, lector, latrare nolito,*
Nam mordere queat dentibus absq; suis.
Vincere si pisces cupias, documenta memento
Aurea, scripta libro commoditate tuâ.

Bark not at Barker, *lest he bite;*
But if in angling thou delight,
To kill the Trout, and cook the Fish,
Follow his rules and have thy wish.

Per Morganum Hoptonum
Armig.

The Art of Angling

The Art of Angling.

Noble Lord,

Under favour I will complement and put a case to your Honour. I met with a man, and upon our discourse he fell out with me, having a good weapon, but neither stomach nor skil; I say this man may come home by Weeping cross, I will cause the Clerk to toll his knell. It is the very like case to the gentleman Angler that goeth to the River for his pleasure: this Angler hath neither judgement nor experience, he may come home light laden at his leisure.

A man that goeth to the River for his pleasure, must understand when he cometh there to set forth his tackle: The first thing he must do, is to observe the Sun and the Wind for day, the

Moon, the Stars, and the wanes of the Aire for night, to set forth his tackles for day or night, and accordingly to go for his pleasure and some profit.

For example. The Sun proves cloudy, then must you set forth either your ground bait tackles, or of the brightest of your flyes. If the Sun prove bright and clear, then must you put on the darkest of your flyes; thus must you to work with your flyes, light for darkness, and dark for lightness, with the wind in the South, which blowes the fly in the Trouts mouth. Though I set down the wind in the South, I am indifferent where the wind standeth, either with ground-bait or menow, so that I can cast my bait into the River. The very same observation is for night as for day; for, if the Moone prove clear, or the Stars glitter in the sky, it is as ill angling that night as if it were high noon in the midst of the summer, when the Sun shineth at the brightest, wherein there is no hopes of pleasure.

I will begin to angle for the Trout, and discourse his qualitie.

The first thing you must gain must be a neat taper rod light before, with a tender hasel top which is very gentle, with a single hair of five lengths long, one tyed to another, for the bottom of my line, and a line of three haired links for the uppermost part, and so you may kill the greatest Trout that swims, with sea-room.

Now I say he that angles with a line made of three haired links for the bottom, and more at the top, may kill fish, but he that angles with a line made of one haired link, shall kill five to the others one; for, the Trout is very quick-sighted, therefore the best way either for night or day is to keep out of sight.

You must angle alwayes with the point of the rod down the stream, for trouts have not quickness of sight so perfect up the stream as they have opposite against them.

But observe the seasonable times. For example, we begin to angle in *March*: if it prove cloudy, you may angle with the ground baits all day long: but if it prove bright and clear, you must take evening and morning, or else you are not like to do good: so times must be observed and truly understood; for when an angler cometh to the River for his pleasure, and doth not understand to set forth his tackles fit for the time, it is as good keep them in the bag as to set them forth.

Now I am determined to angle with the ground baits, and set my tackles to my rod, and go to my pleasure. I begin at the uppermost part of the stream, carrying my line with an upright hand, feeling my plummet running truly on the ground some ten inches from the hook, plumming my line according to the swiftness of the stream I angle in, for one plummet will not serve for all streams; for the true angling is that the plummet run truly on the ground.

For the bait, the red knotted worm is very good, where Brandlins are not to be had; but Brandlins are better.

Now I will shew you how to make these Brandlins fit to angle with, and to make them lusty and fat, that they may live long on the hook, which causeth the best sport; for that is a chief point, and causeth the best sport.

You must take the yolk of an egg, and some eight or ten spoonfulls of the top of new milk, beaten well together in a porringer, warm it a little until you see it curdle, then take it off the fire and set it to cool; when it is cold, take a spoonful and drop it on the moss in an earthen pot, every drop about the bigness of a green pease, shifting your moss twice in the summer, and once a week in the winter. Thus doing, you shall feed your worms and make them fat and lusty, that they will live long and be lusty and lively on your hook. And thus you may keep them all the year long. This is my true experiment for the ground baits, with the running line for the trout.

My Lord, I will now shew the angling with a Menow (called in some places Pincks) for the Trout, which is a pleasant sport, and killeth the greatest fish: The Trout cometh boldly at the bait, as if it were a Mastiffe dog at a Beare; you may angle with greater Tackles and stronger, and be no prejudice in your Angling. A line made of three silks and three hairs twisted for the uppermost part of your line, and a line made of two silks and two hairs twisted for the bottome next your hook, with a swivel nigh the middle of your line, and an indifferent long hook. But if you can attain to angle with a line of foure haired links for the uppermost part, and a line of three haired links for the bottom, for the finer you angle with, it is the better.

Now I must shew you how to bait the menow on your hook: You must put your hook through the lowermost part of the menow's mouth, so draw your hook through; then put the hook in at the mouth again, let the point of the hook come out at the hindmost fin; then draw your line and the menow's mouth will close, that no water get into its belly; you must be alwayes angling with the point of your rod down the stream, drawing your menow up the side of the stream by little & little, nigh the top of the water; the trout seeing the bait, cometh at it most fiercely; give a little time before you strike. This is the true way without lead, for many times I have had them come at the lead and forsake the menow. He that trieth shall prove it in time.

My Lord, I will shew you the way to angle with a flye, which is a delightfull sport.

The rod must be light and tender, if you can fit your self with a hasel of one piece, or of two pieces set together in the most convenient manner, light and gentle. Set your line to your rod, for the uppermost part you may use your own discretion, for the lowermost part next your flye it must be of three or four haired links. If you can attain to angle with a line of one hair, two or three links one tyed to another next your hook, you shall have more rises and kill more fish. Be sure you do not overload your self with lengths of your line. Before you begin to angle make a triall, having the wind on your back, to see at what length you can cast your flye, that the flye light first into the water, and no longer, for if any of the line fall into the water before the flye, it is better uncast than thrown. Be sure you be casting alwayes down the stream with the wind behind you, and the Sun before you. It is a speciall point to have the Sun and moon before you, for the very motion of the rod drives all the pleasure from you, either by day or by night in all your anglings, both with worms and flyes, there must be a great care of that.

Let us begin to angle in March with the flye. If the weather prove windy or cloudy, there are severall kinds of Palmers that are good for that time.

First, a black Palmer ribbed with silver. Secondly, a black Palmer ribbed with an orenge-tawny body. Thirdly, a black Palmer made all of black. Fourthly, a red Palmer ribbed with gold. Fifthly, a red palmer mixed with an orenge tawny body of cruell. All these flyes must be made with hackles, and they will serve all the year long morning and evening, windy or cloudy. Without these flyes you cannot make a dayes angling good. I have heard say that there is for every moneth in the year a flye for that moneth; but that is but talk, for there is but one monethly flye in the yeare, that is the May-flye. Then if the aire prove clear you must imitate the Hawthorn flye, which is all black and very small, the smaller the better. In May take the May flye, imitate that. Some make it with a shammy body, and ribbed with a black hair. Another way it is made with sandy hogs hair ribbed with black silk, and winged with Mallards feathers, according to the fancy of the angler, if he hath judgement. For first, when it comes out of the shell, the flye is somewhat whiter, then afterwards it growes browner, so there is judgement in that. There is another fly called the oak-flye that is a very good flye, which is made of orenge colour cruell and black, with a brown wing, imitate that. There is another flye made with the strain of a Peacocks feather, imitating the Flesh-flye, which is very good in a bright day. The Grasse-hopper which is green, imitate that. The smaller these flyes be made, and of indifferent small hooks, they are the better. These sorts which I have set down will serve all the year long, observing the times and seasons, if the angler have any judgement. Note the lightest of your flies for cloudy and dark, and the darkest of your flyes for the brightest dayes, and the rest for indifferent times; a mans own judgement with some experience must guide him: If he mean to kill fish he must alter his flyes according to these directions. Now of late I have found that hogs wooll of several colours makes good bodies, & the wooll of a red heifer makes a good body, and beares wooll makes a good body: there are many good furres that make good bodies: and now I work much of hogs wooll, for I finde it floateth best and procureth the best sport.

The naturall flye is sure angling, and will kill great store of trouts with much pleasure. As for the May flie you shall have him playing alwayes at the rivers side, especially against rain: the Oak flie is to be had on the but of an oak or an ash, from the beginning of May to the end of August; it is a brownish flie, and standeth alwaies with his head towards the root of the tree, very easie to be found: the small black fly is to be had on every hathorn tree after the buds be come forth: your grasse-hopper which is to be had in any medow of grass in June or July. With these flies you must angle with such a rod as you angle with the ground bait: the line must not be so long as the rod, drawing your flye as you find convenient in your angling! When you come to the deep waters that stand somewhat still, make your line two yards long or thereabouts, and dop or drop your flye behind a bush, which angling I have had good sport at; we call it *dopping*.

My Lord sent to me at Sun going down to provide him a good dish of Trouts against the next morning by sixe of the clock, I went to the door to see how the wanes of the aire were like to prove. I returned answer, that I doubted not, God willing, but to be provided at his time appointed. I went presently to the river, and it proved very dark, I drew out a line of three silks and three hairs twisted for the uppermost part, and a line of two hairs and two silks twisted for the lower part, with a good large hook: I baited my hook with two lob-worms, the four ends hanging as meet as I could guess them in the dark, I fell to angle. It proved very dark, so that I had good sport angling with the lob worms as I do with the flye on the top of the water; you shall hear the fish rise at the top of the water, then you must loose a slack line down to the bottom as nigh as you can guess, then hold your line strait, feeling the fish bite, give time, there is no doubt of losing fish, for there is not one among twenty but doth gorge the bait; the least stroke you can strike fastens the hook and makes the fish sure; letting the fish take a turn or two you may take the fish up with your hands. The night began to alter and grow somewhat lighter, I took off the lob-worms and set to my rod a white

Palmer-flye, made of a large hook; I had sport for the time untill it grew lighter; so I took off the white Palmer and set to a red Palmer made of a large hook; I had good sport untill it grew very light: then I took off the red Palmer and set to a black Palmer; I had good sport, made up the dish of fish. So I put up my tackles and was with my Lord at his time appointed for the service.

These three flyes with the help of the lob-worms serve to angle all the year for the night, observing the times as I have shewed you in this night-work, the white flye for darknesse, the red flye in *medio*, and the black flye for lightnesse. This is the true experience for angling in the night, which is the surest angling of all, and killeth the greatest Trouts. Your lines may be strong, but must not be longer then your rod.

THe rod light and taper, thy tackle fine,
Thy lead ten inches upon the line;
Bigger or lesse, according to the stream,
Angle in the dark, when others dream:
Or in a cloudy day with a lively worm,
The Brandlin is best, but give him a turn
Before thou do land a large wel grown Trout.
And if with a flye thou wilt have about,
Overload not with links, that the flye nay fall

First on the stream, for that's all in all.
The line shorter than the rods, with a naturall flye:
But the chief point of all is the cookery.

Now having taken a good dish of Trouts I presented them to my Lord. He having provided good company, commanded me to turn Cook and dress them for dinner. Whereupon I gave my Lord this bill of fare, which did furnish his table as it was furnished with flesh.

Trouts in broth, which is restorative, which must be boyled in milk, putting to it some large mace, letting it boyle up. Before you put the trouts into the Kettle, the trouts must be drawn and clean washed before you put them in. So keep them with high boyling, untill you think them boyled sufficient. Then you must take a slice or two of good sweet butter and put into your dish, so pour on the broth, having provided the yolks of half a dozen eggs, being very well beaten in a dish or porringer, pour it into your broth, so stir it well; I make no doubt it will be good broth.

The broth eaten, provide for the sauce some butter, the inner part of a lemmon, the yolk of an egge well beaten together, so pour it into the dish, I make no doubt but it will be well liked of. If they doe not like of this broth, when you boyle other trouts for the service, let the trouts be boyled sufficiently in such liquor as I will shew you now following. You may take the quantity of a quart of the top of the liquor with half a pint of Sack, boyle it together, then provide the yolks of halfe a dozen eggs well beaten together; beat all this together with a slice or two of good sweet butter; no doubt but this will be very good.

Now we must have two dishes of calvored Trouts hot. For the first course the sauce shall be butter and vinegar, 2 or 3 Anchoves, the bones taken out, beaten together with the yolk of one egge for one of the dishes, with a lemmon squeezed on them. For the other dish the sauce and purtenances shall be a quart of oysters stewed in half a pint of Whitewine, so put on the fish, then butter and vinegar being well beaten, with the yolk of an egge poured on that, squeezing a lemmon on the fish, there is no doubt but they will be eaten with delight.

Out of this kettle we must have two dishes to eat cold for the latter course.

First I will shew you the punctuall boyling and calvoring of four dishes.

You must draw out the entrails of the fish, cutting the fish two or three times crosse the backe, lay them on a tray or platter, sprinkle a little salt on them, you must have a quart of vinegar put in a skellet and let it boyle, when it boyles take it off the fire and pour it upon your fish, you shall see your fish rise presently, if they be new, and there is no doubt of calvoring; you must put so much water in your kettle as you think will cover them; you must put in a handful of salt, some rosemary, thyme, and sweet marjoram in a bunch; then you must make this liquor boyle with a fierce fire made of wood: when the liquor hath boyled very well, put in your fish by and by untill you have put in all, keeping them boyling, having provided a cover for your kettle, so put on the cover; you must have a pair of bellows to blow up your fire with speed, that the liquor may boyl up to the top of the kettle, then put in the vinegar that you poured on them before you put them into the kettle, then blow up your liquor with a fierce fire, for the fierce boyling makes the fish to calvor: if the fish be new killed you may let them boyle a quarter of an hour; when they are cold you may put them into a tray or earthen pan, and make such use of them as you have for the the other services, and the rest you may put into a pan untill you have oo-casion to use them; be sure they lie covered in the liquor they were boyled in. First put in the one Trout: let one blow up the fire untill the liquor boyle, then put in another; so do untill all are in and boyled.

We must have one dish of Broyled Trouts, when the in-trails be taken out, you must cut them across the side: being washed clean, you must take some sweet herbs, as thyme, sweet marjoram, and parlsey chopped very small, the trouts being cut somewhat thick, and fill the cuts full with the chopt herbs, then make your gridiron fit to put them on, being well cooked with rough suet, then lay the Trouts on a charcoal-fire: as you turn them bast them with fresh butter untill you think they are well broyled: the sauce must be butter and vinegar, the yolk of an egge beaten, beat all together and put it on the fish for the service.

To fry a dish of Trouts you must take such a quantity of suet as you shall think sufficient to fry them, and put it in your pan, and be sure that it boyle before you put in your fish, being cut on the side and floured, you must keep them with sitting all the time you are frying them: being fryed sufficiently, when you have dished them the sauce must be butter, vinegar, and some lemmon, but very small, and beaten with your butter and vinegar, then poured on your fish for the service.

The best dish of stewed fish that ever I heard commended of the English, was dressed this way: First they were broiled on a charcoale fire, being cut on the side as fried Trouts, then the stwe pan was taken and set on a chaffingdish of coles, there was put into the stew-pan half a pound of sweet butter, one peniworth of beaten cinnamon, a little vinegar; when all was melted the fish was put into the pan, and covered with a covering plate, so kept stewing half an hour, being turned, then taken out of the stew-pan and dished, be sure to beat your sauce before you put it on your fish, then squeeze a lemmon on your fish: it was the best dish of fish that ever I heard commended by Noblemen and Gentlemen. This is our English fashion.

There are divers wayes of stewing; this which I set down last was the English way: But note this, that your stewed trouts must be cut on the side: you may make a dish of stwewed trouts out of your boyling kettle, stewing of them with the same materialls as I did the broiled trouts, I dare warrant them good meat, and to be very well liked.

The Italian he stews upon a chaffing-dish of coles, with whitewine, cloves and mace, nutmegs sliced, a little ginger; you must understand when this fish is stewed, the same liquor that the fish is stewed in must be beaten with some sweet butter and juice of a lemmon, before it is dished for the service. The French doth adde to this a slice or two of bacon, Though I have been no traveller I may speak it, for I have been admitted into the most Ambassadors Kitchins that have come into England this forty years, and do wait on them stil at the Lord Protector's charge, and am paid duly for it: for sometimes I see slovenly scullions abuse good fish most grosly.

We must have a Trout pie to eat hot, and another to eat cold: the first thing you must gain must be a peck of the best wheaten flower, two pound of butter, two quarts of milk new from the Cow, half a dozen of eggs to make the past. Where I was born there is not a girle of ten yeares of age, but can make a pie.

For one pie, the trouts shall be opened, and the guts taken out and clean washed, seasoned with pepper and salt, then laid in the pie, half a pound of currans put among the fish with a pound of sweet butter cut in pieces, and set on the fish, so close it up; when it is baked and come out of the oven, pour into the pie three or four spoonfulls of claret wine, so dish it and serve to the table. These trouts shall eat moist and close.

For the other pie the trouts shall be broyled a little, it will make the fish rise and eat more crisp: season them with pepper and salt and lay them in the pie: you must put more butter in this pie than the other, for this will keep, and must be filled up with butter when it cometh forth of the oven.

There is one good trout of a good length, some eighteen or twentry inches long, we will have that rosted.

You must take out the intrails of this trout with opening the trout one inch at the upper end of his belly, as nigh the gills as you can; then open the trout within one inch of the vent, so you may take the intailes clean out: then wash the trout very clean, keeping the belly whole: then take half a pound of sweet butter, some thyme, sweet marjoram and parsley chopt very small, mix the butter and herbs together and put them into his belly, with half a dozen of oysters, sew up the two slits wih a needle and thred as well as you can: there are broches made to rost a fish, for want of that broch you must take an ordinary broch and spit the fish on; take four or five small laths full the length of the fish, tie those laths on about the fish with a piece of packthred from one end to the other, make the fish fast on the spit, set the spit to the fire; the first thing you bast the fish with must be a little claret wine, next you must bast with butter, with an anchovas beaten together, then bast with the liquor that falleth from the fish untill the fish is rosted; when the fish is rosted take a warm dish and cut the fish off into that dish; then beat the sauce that came from the fish very well, and pour it on the fish, and serve it up.

I will shew you the way to *marionate* a trout or other fish, that it shall keep a quarter of a year in the heat of summer, which is the Italians rarest dish for fresh fish, and will eat perfect and sweet.

You must take out the intrailes and cut them on the side as you do to fry: being washed clean and dried with a cloth, lay them on a tray or board, sprinkle a little salt on them, flower them as to fry them, so take your frying pan with so much suet as when it is melted the fish may lie up to the mid-sides in the liquor, fry them, and every time you turn them flower again, untill you finde that they are fried sufficiently: when you think the fish is dried, take it out of the pan and lay it upon something that the liquor may drein out of it: when the fish is cold you may rear it on end; you must provide a close vessel to keep this fish and liquor in, that no wind can come in, according to the quantity you make triall of; the liquor must be half claretwine, the other half vinegar, two or three bay leaves, so much saffron as a nut tied in a cloth, with some cloves and large mace, and some nutmegs sliced: boyl all this together very well, when the liquor is cold and the fish cold put the liquor into a close vessell, and put the fish into it, then slice three or four lemmons and lay among your fish, make all close that no wind can come into the vessell. After eight or ten dayes you may begin to eat of this fish; the sauce to eat with this fish must be some of the same liquor with some of the sliced lemmon. You must understand that this fish must have a little time before it will come to his kind.

REstorative broth of Trouts learne to make:
Some fry and some stew, and some also bake.
First broyl and then bake, is a rule of good skill,
And when thou dost fortune a great trout to kill,
Then rost him, and baste first with good claret wine,
But the colvor'd boyl'd trout will make thee to dine
With dainty contentment, both the hot and the cold,
And the marrienate Trout I dare to be bold
For a quarter of a year wil keep to thy mind,
If covered close & preserved from wind.
But mark well good brother, what now I doe say,
Sauce made of Anchoves is an excellent way,
With oysters and lemmon, clove, nutmeg and mace,
When the brave spotted trout hath been boyled apace
With many sweet herbs: for forty years I
In Ambassadours Kitchins learn'd my cookery.
The French and Italian no better can doe,
Observe well my rules and you'l say so too.

I will now shew you the way to take a *Salmon.*

THe first thing you must gain must be a rod of some ten foot in the stock, that will carry a top of six foot pretty stiffe and strong, the reason is, because there must be a little wire ring at the upper end of the top for the line to run through, that you may take up and loose the line at your pleasure; you must have your winder within two foot of the bottom to goe on your rod made in this manner, with a spring, that you may put it on as low as you please.

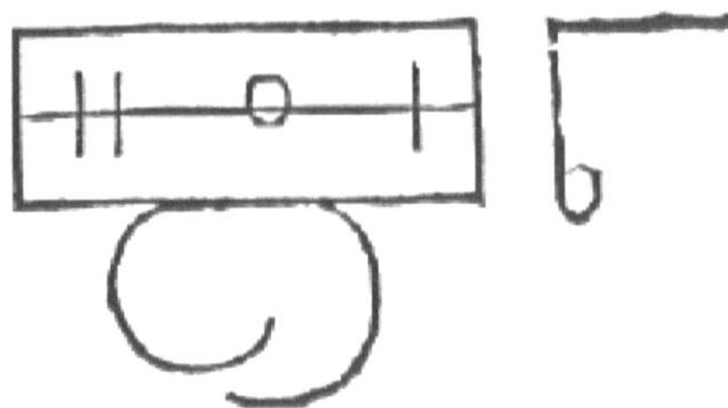

The Salmon swimmeth most commonly in the midst of the river. In all his travells his desire is to see the uppermost part of the river, travelling on his journey in the heat of the day he may take a bush; if the fisherman espy him, he goeth at him with his speare, so shortneth his journey.

The angler that goeth to catch him with a line and hook, must angle for him as nigh the middle of the water as he can with one of these baits: He must take two lob-worms baited as handsomly as he can, that the four ends may hang meet of a length, and so angle as nigh the bottom as he can, feeling your plummet run on the ground some twelve inches from the hook: if you angle for him with a flie (which he will rise at like a Trout) the flie must be made of a large hook, which hook must carry six wings, or four at least; there is judgement in making those flyes. The Salmon will come at a Gudgeon in the manner of a trouling, and cometh at it bravely, which is fine angling for him and good. You must be sure that you have your line of twenty six yards of length, that you may have your convenient time to turne him, or else you are in danger to lose him: but if you turn him you are very like to have the fish with small tackles: the danger is all in the running out both of Salmon and Trout, you must forecast to turn the fish as you do a wild horse, either upon the right or the left hand, & wind up your line as you finde occasion in the guiding the fish to the shore, having a good large landing hook to take him up.

This fish being killed, if it be not boyled well, then all your labor and pains is lost. If you boyl the fish whole, you must take out the intrailes, cutting the fish three or four times crosse the back, and an inch along the back three or four times crossing the former cuts; by that reason you shall see whether he calvors or no. then you must take a tray according to the length of the Salmon, being dried with a clean cloth; then you must take the Salmon and lay it on the tray, so salt the fish within and without with an indifferent hand, that will give a good relish. Then you must take a quart of the best whitewine vinegar and put it in a skellet and set it on the fire, and let it boyle well and high, so pour it all along on your Salmon, you shall see the Salmon rise presently, and very like to calvor, if the Salmon be new killed, so let it lie untill you are ready to spend it. Then you must take such a pan or kettle that you think the Salmon will lie well in, and set it on the fire made of good drie faggots, and put so much water in the pan or kettle as you think will cover the fish and no more, with two or three handfulls of salt, one pint of vinegar, a good bunch of rosemary, thyme and sweet marjoram tied together, make this liquor boyle very high, then put in your Salmon, having a good paire of bellowes to blow up your fire that the liquor may boyle with speed, then put the vinegar in that was put on the Salmon first, make it boyle up presently, so take your cover and put on, keeping the liquor and Salmon boyling with a fierce fire nigh the space of an hour. If you chine the Salmon and cut the fish in pieces, somewhat lesse boyling will serve. If you keep it to eat cold you must put the liquor and fish all cold together, and make it close, that as little wind come in as you can. If you will eat any of this hot, the sauce is butter, a little vinegar, a lemmon shred very small, beaten together, then the yolks of two eggs beaten & put in the sauce, & beaten very well all together; so being dished pour it on the fish and serve it up to the table, I do not doubt but the dish will be well liked.

CLose to the botom in the midst of the water
I fished for a Salmon and there I caught her.
My Plummet twelve inches from the large hook,
Two lob-wormes hang'd equall, which she never forsook.
Nor yet the great hook with the six winged flye,
And she makes at a gudgeon most furiously.
My strong line was just twenty six yards long,
I gave him a turne though I found him strong.
I wound up my tackle to guide him to shore;
The landing hook helps much, the cookery more.

N O W we will see whether we can take a Pike.

There was one of my name the best Trouler for a Pike within this Realm of England: the manner of his trouling was with a hasell rod some twelve foot long, with a ring of wire in the top of the rod for his line to run through: within two foot of the bottom of the rod there was a hole made to put in a winder to turn with a barrell, to gather up his line and loose it at his pleasure. This was his manner of trouling with a small fish.

There are severall other wayes to take Pikes.

There is a way to take a Pike, which is called *the taking a Pike by snap,* for which angling you must have a pretty strong rod, for you must angle with a line no longer than your rod, which must be very strong, that you may hold the fish to it; your hook must be strong and armed with wire of two lengths long: you must bait the fish with the head upwards, and the point must come forth of his side a little above his vent. In all your baitings for a Pike you must enter the needle where the point cometh forth, so draw your arming through untill the hook lieth according as you think fit, them make it fast with a little thred to the wire, so fall to work: the bait must be a Gudgeon if you can get it, or a small Trout, which is the best, or else some other small fish.

Now I will pawn my credit that I will shew a way either in mayre, or pond, or river, that shall take more pikes than any trouler shall do with his rod. And thus it is: First take a forked stick, a line of twelve yards long wound upon it. At the upper end leave a yard either to tie a bunch of fags or a bladder to boy up the fish, to carry the bait from the ground, that the fish may swim clear. The bait must be a live fish, either dace, gudgeon, or roche, or a small trout. The forked stick must have a slit on the one side of the fork, that you may put the line in, that the live fish may swim at that gage you set the fish to swim at, that when the Pike taketh the bait, the Pike may have the full liberty of the line for his feed; you may turne all these loose, either in pond or river all day long, the more the better, and do it in a pond with the wind: at night set a small weight, such as may stay the boy, as a ship lieth at anchor, untill the fish feedeth: for the river you must turn all loose with the stream, two or three be sufficient to shew pleasure. Gaged at such a depth they will goe current down the stream: there is no doubt of pleasure if there be Pikes; the hooks must be double hooks, the shanks must be somewhat shorter than ordinary. My reason is, the shorter the hooks be in the shank, it will hurt the live fish the lesse, and it must be armed with small wire well seasoned: But I hold a hook armed with twisted silk to be better, for it will hurt the live fish the lesse. If you arme your hook with wire, the needle must be made with a hook at the end thereof: if you arm your hook with silk, if it be double the same needle will serve; but if you arm the hook single, the needle must be made with an eye, and then you must take one of the baits alive, which you can get, and with one of your needles enter the fish within a straw breadth of the gill; so put the needle in betwixt the skin & the fish, then put the needle out at the hindmost fin, and so to come forth at the gill, then put on the hook, and it will hurt the live fish the lesse: so knit the arming with the live fish to the line, then put off either in maire or pond, with the wind, in the river, with the stream, the more you put of them in the maire, you are like to have the more pleasure: for the river three or four will be sufficient.

There is a time when pikes go a frogging, and also to sun themselves, there is a speedy way to take them, and not to misse one in twenty. You must take a line made of good twisted thred of some six or eight foot long; arm a large hook of some two inches in the bent betwixt beard and bent, arme it to your line, lead the shank of the hook very handsome, that it may guide the hook at your pleasure; you may strike the Pike where you please, as you see good, with the bare hook. This line and hook doth goe beyond all snaring.

The principall sport to take a Pike is to take a Goose, or Gander, or Duck, take one of the Pikes lines, as I have shewed you before, tie the line under the left wing and over the right wing, as a man weareth his belt, turne the Goose off in a pond where Pikes are, there is no doubt of pleasure betwixt the Goose and the Pike. It is the greatest pleasure that a noble Gentleman in Shropshire giveth his friends for entertainment. There is no question among all this fishing but we shall take a brace of good Pikes.

I will now shew you the way to dresse them.

The first thing you must doe when the Pike comes in the Kitchin, if it be alive, is to knock the Pike in the head, that the Pike may bleed, then take an handfull of salt and water, so rub him and scoure him to take the slime off, or else there will be durty meat; then take out the intrailes, cut the Pike crosse the back two or three times, salt it well within and without, set on your Kettle with so much water as will cover the Pike, put in three or four handfulls of salt, some good rosemary, thyme, sweet marjoram, tied together, three or 4 onions, so make your liquor boyle very high with a good fire made of dry faggots, then put in your pike, having your bellowes to blow up the fire that the liquor may boyle up to the top of the Kettle for the space of half an hour, by that time it may be boyled sufficiently; then take the Kettle off the fire, then provide a quart of oysters and stew them in half a pint of white-wine; then take half a pound of good butter, you make take a little of the liquor off the top of the Kettle, beat the butter and liquor together with 2 or 3 anchoves, the skin taken off and the bones taken out, with a piece of lemmon chopped very small, beat all these together, beat the yolk of an egge & put it into the sauce, then beat all together, so dish your Pike, put the oysters on first, then pour on your sauce, there is no doubt but it will be good victualls.

In the Country where I was born we had spits made of iron to rost a Pike or a Carp; you must take water and salt and rub the fish well to take the slime off. To take the intrailes out you must open the fish, cutting the fish an inch in the uppermost part of the belly, and one inch at the vent, so you may take out the intrailes and keep the belly whole: wash the Pike cleane, take halfe a pound of sweet butter, mix the butter with sweet herbs well chopped, put in the Pikes belly with halfe a dozen of oysters, make your cuts as close as you can. For want of such a broch you must have four or five thin laths, so tie the fish on with some packthred from one end to the other, so set your spit to the fire to rost; when it begins to dry a little, take three or four spoonfulls of Claret wine, and baste it first therewith, then take a quarter of a pound of good butter and melt it in a porringer; take two or three anchoves, the skin taken off and bones taken out, beat the butter and anchoves together untill the anchoves be dissolved, then baste the fish with that next, so baste all along with that liquor that falleth from the fish, then warme the dish that must goe to the table, and cut the packthred and let it fall into that dish, so take the liquor that is fallen from the fish and beat it very well together, and pour it on the fish, squeezing a lemon or two on the fish, no doubt but the fish will be eaten and wel liked.

A Rod twelve foot long, and a ring of wire,
A winder and barrell will help thy desire
In killing a Pike, but the forked stick
With a slit and a bladder, and that other fine trick,
Which our Artists call Snap, with a Goose or a Duck,
Will kil two for one if thou have any luck.
The Gentry of Shropshire do merrily smile,
To see a Goose and a belt the fish to beguile.
When a Pike suns himselfe and a frogging doth go,
The two inched hook is better I know
Than the ord'nary snaring: but still I must cry
When the Pike is at home minde the cookery.

To take a Carp either in pond or river, if you mean to have sport with some profit, you must take a peck of ale graines and a good quantity of blood, so mix the the blood and graines together, casting it in the place where you mean to angle; this will gather all the scale-fish together, as Carp, Tench, Roch, Dace, and Bream. The next morning be at your sport very early: plumme your ground, you may angle for the Carp with stronger tackles than ordinary, with a strong line; for your roch and Dace you must angle with fine tackles as single haired lines, if you mean to have sport: the bait must be either a knotted worme or paste for a Carp, but for your Roch and Dace your bait must be either wormes, paste, or gentles, or cadice, or a flye. There is no doubt of sport.

LAte in the evening the ale graines and blood,
Being well mixt together is bait very good
For Carp, Tench and Roch, and Dace to prepare,
If early in the morning at the river you are.
Strong tackle for Carp; for Roch and Dace fine,
Will help thee with fish sufficient for to dine.
For the Carp let thy bait the knotted worm be,
The rest love the cadice, the paste and the flye.

To take a Perch, The Perch feeds well if you light where they be, and biteth very free. My opinion with some experience is to feed with lob-worms chopped in pieces over night; so in the morning betimes, plumming your ground, gaging your line, bait with a red knotted worm, but I hold a menow to be better to bait: put your hook in at the back of the menow betwixt the flesh & the skin, that the menow may swim up and down, your line being boyed up with a cork or quill, that the menow may swim up and down a foot from the ground, there is no doubt of sport and profit.

For the *Chub* and *Barbell* I have no minde to spend much time, because I do not love them, the reason is, because the fish is very full of bones, and in my opinion they are good no way but baked in a pot, putting into the pot half a pint of Claret to dissolve the bones, and then you may eat them somewhat safely. For the Chub you may angle with a flye or a black snaile; and if you take him, if you do not like that way of dressing, you may slit the fish along the back, the scales being taken off, and the intrails taken out, and flower it, so fry it: see whether this dressing is better than baking. A good sauce may make the fish eat better: the sauce is butter, a little vinegar, with a lemmon chopped very small, beaten well together. This may make the fish eat the better.

For the Barbell, I have taken great ones in *Ware* river with wormes, for I know no better bait than wormes: you have a kind of fishing for them at *London* bridge with three or four hooks fixt to a line with a great plummet, so scratch for them. I was acquainted with *Nicholas Harridans* that lived nigh Algate, who hath killed many a dish of Barbells that way with scratching, and he would tell me that they were good souced & no other way, but I have eaten some boyled, but I did not fancy them.

The *Gudgeon* is a dainty fish to eat being dressed when they are new taken, either fried or boyled, and bites very well. If you come where they are you must angle for them with fine tackle, plummed, that your bait goeth nigh the ground with cork or quill: for the bait, there is a worm which is a little short worme, and is called a Gild-taile, which is the best bait I know for them. For the dressing, you may take your choice, either boyled or fryed; the sauce is butter and a little vinegar, to give the relish, well beaten together, with a little piece of a lemmon to squeeze on them. I make no question but you will like them well.

There are many wayes to take *Eeles:* I will shew you a good way to take a dish of Eeles. When you stay a night or two to angle in a river or pond, take four or five lines of some twelve or fourteen yards long, & every two yards make a noose to hang a hook armed with double thred, for it is better than wire. Bait your hooks with millers thumbs, loaches, menows, or gudgons, tie to every line a hook baited. The lines must be laid cross the river in the deepest places, either with stones or pegged, so that the line lay close to the bottom of the river, there is no doubt of taking a dish of Eeles. You must have a small needle with an eye to bait your hooks.

There is a fish in my Countrey (*viz.* Shropshire) called a *Grayling,* which swimmeth in the gallant river of *Severn,* and all the summer lie in the shallow streams of the River, and cometh very free at the top of the water, with much delight and profit. The manner of angling for him is with a good long rod with casting. The bait must be either a small artificiall or a nature flye. The oak flye is easie to be had there, either on the butt of an oak or the butt of an ash. Sometimes these flyes will not be found, then you must provide some cod bait, they lie in a gravelly husk under stones in most small rivers. The May-flye breedeth on that worm, and doth continue until the end of May. This fish is a dainty eating fish; you may make as many good eating dishes of it as of a Trout, four severall wayes.

Now the way to angle with the Cod bait (as we call it) but named here a cadice, is as followeth.

You must angle with a long rod, but light, your line somewhat longer than the rod. The Grayling feedeth at the top of the water. You must have a little float of cork so big around as a hasell nut, when the fish taketh the bait he flyeth away, so that you shall see the cork flee after the fish, then strike; but you must consider this angling is without lead.

We have Fishermen in that Countrey that will go thirty or forty miles by land, and carry their boat on their back, and so angle down all the way home, with this way of angling, providing a little weele made of wicker to carry their fish, so that they will bring home all their fish alive, whereby they make a very profitable journey.

There comes an honest Gentleman, a familiar freind to me, he was an angler, begins to complement with me and asked me how I did, and when I had been angling, and demanded in discourse, what was the reason I did not relate in my book the dressing of his dish of fish which he loved; I pray you sir, said I, what dish of Trouts was that? He said it was a dish of close boyled Trouts buttered with eggs. My answer was to him, that every scullion dresseth that dish against his will, because he cannot calvor them; I will tell you in short: Put your Trouts into the Kettle when the Kettle is set on the fire, and let them boyle gently, as many Cooks doe, and they shall boyle close enough, which is a good dish buttered with eggs, good for ploughmen, but not for the palate. Sir, I hope I have given you satisfaction.

Now, I will shew you how to make flyes. Learn to make two flyes and make all, that is, the Palmer ribbed with gold or silver, and the Mayflye. These are the ground of all flyes.

We will begin to make the Palmer-flye. You must arm your line on the in-side your hook, then take your sizzers and cut so much of the browne of the Mallards feather as in your owne reason shall make the wings, then lay the outermost part of the feather near the hook, and the point of the feather next toward the shank of the hook, so whip it three or four times about the hook with the same silk you armed the hook with , so make your silk fast; then you must take the hackle of a cock or capon, or a plovers top feather, then take the hackle, silk, or cruell, gold or silver thred, make all fast at the bent of the hook, then begin to work with the cruell, and silver thred, work it up to the wings, every bout shifting your fingers and making a stop, then the cruell and silver will fall right, then make fast, then work up the hackle to the same place, then make the hackle fast; then you must take the hook betwixt your fingers and thumb in the left hand, with a needle or pin part the wings in two, so take the silk you have wrought with all this while, and whip once about the shank that falleth crosse betwixt the wings; than with your thumb you must turn the point of the feather towards the bent of the hook, so view the proportion.

For other flyes, if you make the grounds of hogs wooll, sandy, or black, or white, or the wooll of a beare, or of a two-year old red bullock; you must work all the grounds upon a waxed silk, then you must arm and set on the wings, as I have shewed you before.

For the May-flye, you must work with some of these grounds, which it is very good ribbed with a black hair; you may work the body with a cruell, imitating the colour, or with silver suitable to the wings.

For the oak-flie, you must take orenge-colour tawny, and black for the body, and the browne of the Mallards feather for the wings. If you do after my directions they will kill fish, observing the times fitting, and following former directions.

If any worthy or honest Angler cannot hit of these my directions, let him come to me, he shall read and I will work, he shall see all things done according to my foresaid directions. So I conclude for the flye, having shewed you my true experience.

A *Brother of the Angle must alwaies be sped*
With three black Palmers, & also two red,
And all made with Hackles: in a cloudy day,
Or in windy weather, angle you may:
But morning and evening, if the day be bright,
And the chief point of all is to keep out of sight.
In the moneth of May, none but the May-flye;
For every month one, is a pitiful lye:
The black hawthorn flye must be very small,
And the sandy hogs haire is sure best of all
For the Mallard wing'd May-flye; and the Peacocks train
Will look like the flesh-flye to kill Trout amaine.
The oak flye is good, if it have a brown wing,
So is the Grashopper that in July doth sing,

With a green body, make him on a midle siz'd hook;
But when you have catcht fish, then play the good Cook.
Once more my good brother, Ile speak in thy eare,
Hogs, red Cows, & Bears wooll, to float best appear,
And so doth your fur, if rightly it fall;
But alwayes remember, make two and make all.

I could set down as many wayes to dress Eeles as would furnish a Lords table, but I will relate but one.

Take off the skin whole untill you come within two inches of the taile; beginning at the head take out the intrailes, wash the eele clean, dry it with a cloth, scotch it all along on both the sides; take some pepper and salt, mix them together, rub the Eele very well with the pepper and salt; draw the skin on again whole, tie the skin about the head with a little thred lapped round; it must be broyled on a charcole fire, let your gridiron be hot, rub your gridiron well with rough suet, then the skin will neither break nor burn. The Eele will broyl in his own liquor, and will be a good dish. But, take the skin off and stew the Eele betwixt two dishes upon a chaffindish of coles, with sweet butter, a little vinegar, with some beaten cinnamon, that will be a rare dish.

The boyling of a Carp is the very same way as I have shewed you for the Trout, with the scales on; no better sauce can be made than anchoves sauce: The high boyling is the best for all fresh-water fish. I have served seven times seven years to see the experiment.

If you desire to make your sauce black, if your Carp be alive, you must take your knife and thrust it about the middle of his belly, then the Carp will bleed; so take a little vinegar and put it in a saucer, and as the blood falleth in stir it about untill all the blood is run. If the Carp be dead, take the cold blood out of the Carp and beat it with your sauce. This is called *black sauce for a Carp.*

If there be any Gentleman that liveth adjoyning to a river side where Trouts are, I will shew him the way to bring them to feed that he may see them at his pleasure. And to bring store to the place, gather great garden-worms, the quantity of a pint or a quart, chop them in pieces and throw them where you intend to have your pleasure; with feeding often there is no doubt of their coming, they will come as sheep to the pen; you must begin to feed with pieces of worms by hand by one and one, untill you see them feed; then you may feed with liver and lights, so your pleasure will be effected.

I have a willing mind with Gods help to preserve all those that love this recreation, to goe dry in their boots and shooes, to preserve their healths, which one receit is worth much more than this book will cost.

First, they must take a pint of Linseed oyle, with half a pound of mutton suet, six or eight ounces of bees wax, and half a pinniworth of rosin, boyle all this in a pipkin together, so let it coole untill it be milk warm, then take a little hair brush and lay it on your new boots; but its best that this stuff be laid on before the boot-maker makes the boots, then brush them once over after they come from him; as for old boots you must lay it on when your boots be dry.

If you want good Tackles of all sorts, you must go to Mr. *Oliver Fletcher* at the west end of Pauls, at the sign of the three Trouts.

If you would have the best Hooks of all sorts, go to *Charles Kirby,* who lives in shooe lane at Harp alley, in Mill-yard.

If you would have a rod to beare and to sit neatly, you must go to *John Hobs* who liveth at the sign of the George behind the Mews by Charing-crosse.

A *Live and small minow is the best bait*
  To kill a great Pearch by Anglers deceit,
A black snaile is the bait for the bonny Chub,
  A Barbell souced is meat very good.
The greedy Gudgeon doth Love the Gild taile,
  And the twelve yard line doth never faile,
To kill of good Eees an excellent dish,
  With nooses and baits of the little fish;
At the but of the oak take you the flye,
  And kill the Grayling immediately.
But when of all sorts thou hast thy wish,
  Follow Barkers *advice to cook the fish.*
Think then of the gatehouse, for neere it lives he,
  Who kindly will teach thee to make the flye.
And if thou live by a river side,
  Believe thou thy friend who often hath try'd,
And brought store of fish, as sheep to the pen;
  But friend, let me tell thee once agen,
His art to keep thee both warm and dry,
  Deserveth thy love perpetually.
He names three men to thee, like a good friend,
  Make use of them all, and so I end.

Noble Lord,

I *Have found an experience of late, which you may angle with, and take* great *store of this kind of fish: first, it is the best bait for a Trout that I have sen in all my time, and will take great store, and not faile, if they be there. Secondly, it is a speciall bait for Dace, or Dare, good for Chub, or Bottlin, or Grayling. The bait is the roe of a Salmon, or Trout, if it be a large Trout, that the spawnes be any thing great. You must angle for the Trout with this bait as you angle with the brandlin, taking a paire of cisers and cut so much as a large Hasel nut, and bait your hook, so fall to your sport, there is no doubt of pleasure. If I had known it it but twenty years agoe I would have gained a hundred pounds onely with that bait.I am bound in duty to divulge it to your Honour, and not to carry it to my grave with me. I do desire that men of quality should have it that delight in that pleasure: The greedy Angler will murmur at me, but for that I care not.*

For the angling for the scale-fish they must angle either with cork or quill, plumming their ground, and with feeding with the same bait, taking them asunder that they may spread abrod that the fish may feed and come to your place. there is no doubt of pleasure angling with fine Tackles, as single haire lines at least five or six lengths long, a small hook with two or three spawns, the bait will hold one week. If you keep it on any longer, you must hang it up to dry a little: When you go to your pleasure again, put the bait in a little water, it will come in again.

Sic vale feliciter.

Thomas Barker.

Also from Benediction Books ...

Wandering Between Two Worlds: Essays on Faith and Art
Anita Mathias
Benediction Books, 2007
152 pages
ISBN: 0955373700

Available from www.amazon.com, www.amazon.co.uk
www.wanderingbetweentwoworlds.com

In these wide-ranging lyrical essays, Anita Mathias writes, in lush, lovely prose, of her naughty Catholic childhood in Jamshedpur, India; her large, eccentric family in Mangalore, a sea-coast town converted by the Portuguese in the sixteenth century; her rebellion and atheism as a teenager in her Himalayan boarding school, run by German missionary nuns, St. Mary's Convent, Nainital; and her abrupt religious conversion after which she entered Mother Teresa's convent in Calcutta as a novice. Later rich, elegant essays explore the dualities of her life as a writer, mother, and Christian in the United States--Domesticity and Art, Writing and Prayer, and the experience of being "an alien and stranger" as an immigrant in America, sensing the need for roots.

About the Author

Anita Mathias was born in India, has a B.A. and M.A. in English from Somerville College, Oxford University and an M.A. in Creative Writing from the Ohio State University. Her essays have been published in The Washington Post, The London Magazine, The Virginia Quarterly Review, Commonweal, Notre Dame Magazine, America, The Christian Century, Religion Online, The Southwest Review, Contemporary Literary Criticism, New Letters, The Journal, and two of HarperSanFrancisco's The Best Spiritual Writing anthologies. Her non-fiction has won fellowships from The National Endowment for the Arts; The Minnesota State Arts Board; The Jerome Foundation, The Vermont Studio Center; The Virginia Centre for the Creative Arts, and the First Prize for the Best General Interest Article from the Catholic Press Association of the United States and Canada. Anita has taught Creative Writing at the College of William and Mary, and now lives and writes in Oxford, England.

"Yesterday's Treasures for Today's Readers"
Titles by Benediction Classics available from Amazon.co.uk

Religio Medici, Hydriotaphia, Letter to a Friend, Thomas Browne

Pseudodoxia Epidemica: Or, Enquiries into Commonly Presumed Truths, Thomas Browne

Urne Buriall and The Garden of Cyrus, Thomas Browne

The Maid's Tragedy, Beaumont and Fletcher

The Custom of the Country, Beaumont and Fletcher

Philaster Or Love Lies a Bleeding, Beaumont and Fletcher

A Treatise of Fishing with an Angle, Dame Juliana Berners.

Pamphilia to Amphilanthus, Lady Mary Wroth

The Compleat Angler, Izaak Walton

The Magnetic Lady, Ben Jonson

Every Man Out of His Humour, Ben Jonson

The Masque of Blacknesse. The Masque of Beauty,. Ben Jonson

The Life of St. Thomas More, William Roper

Pendennis, William Makepeace Thackeray

Salmacis and Hermaphroditus attributed to Francis Beaumont

Friar Bacon and Friar Bungay Robert Greene

Holy Wisdom, Augustine Baker

The Jew of Malta and the Massacre at Paris, Christopher Marlowe

Tamburlaine the Great, Parts 1 & 2 AND Massacre at Paris, Christopher Marlowe

All Ovids Elegies, Lucans First Booke, Dido Queene of Carthage, Hero and Leander, Christopher Marlowe

The Titan, Theodore Dreiser

Scapegoats of the Empire: The true story of the Bushveldt Carbineers, George Witton

All Hallows' Eve, Charles Williams

The Place of The Lion, Charles Williams

The Greater Trumps, Charles Williams

My Apprenticeship: Volumes I and II, Beatrice Webb

Last and First Men / Star Maker, Olaf Stapledon

Last and First Men, Olaf Stapledon

Darkness and the Light, Olaf Stapledon

The Worst Journey in the World, Apsley Cherry-Garrard

The Schoole of Abuse, Containing a Pleasaunt Invective Against Poets, Pipers, Plaiers, Iesters and Such Like Catepillers of the Commonwelth, Stephen Gosson

Russia in the Shadows, H. G. Wells

Wild Swans at Coole, W. B. Yeats

A hundreth good pointes of husbandrie, Thomas Tusser

The Collected Works of Nathanael West: "The Day of the Locust", "The Dream Life of Balso Snell", "Miss Lonelyhearts", "A Cool Million", Nathanael West

Miss Lonelyhearts & The Day of the Locust, Nathaniel West

The Worst Journey in the World, Apsley Cherry-Garrard

Scott's Last Expedition, V1, R. F. Scott

The Dream of Gerontius, John Henry Newman

The Brother of Daphne, Dornford Yates

The Downfall of Robert Earl of Huntington, Anthony Munday

Clayhanger, Arnold Bennett

The Regent, A Five Towns Story Of Adventure In London , Arnold Bennett

The Card, A Story Of Adventure In The Five Towns , Arnold Bennett

South: The Story of Shackleton's Last Expedition 1914-1917, Sir Ernest Shackketon

Greene's Groatsworth of Wit: Bought With a Million of Repentance, Robert Greene

Beau Sabreur, Percival Christopher Wren

The Hekatompathia, or Passionate Centurie of Love, Thomas Watson

The Art of Rhetoric, Thomas Wilson

Stepping Heavenward, Elizabeth Prentiss

Barker's Delight, or The Art of Angling, Thomas Barker

The Napoleon of Notting Hill, G.K. Chesterton

The Douay-Rheims Bible (The Challoner Revision)

Endimion - The Man in the Moone, John Lyly

Gallathea and Midas, John Lyly,

Mother Bombie, John Lyly

Manners, Custom and Dress During the Middle Ages and During the Renaissance Period, Paul Lacroix

Obedience of a Christian Man, William Tyndale

St. Patrick for Ireland, James Shirley

The Wrongs of Woman; Or Maria/Memoirs of the Author of a Vindication of the Rights of Woman, Mary Wollstonecraft and William Godwin

De Adhaerendo Deo. Of Cleaving to God, Albertus Magnus

Obedience of a Christian Man, William Tyndale

A Trick to Catch the Old One, Thomas Middleton

The Phoenix, Thomas Middleton

A Yorkshire Tragedy, Thomas Middleton (attrib.)

The Princely Pleasures at Kenelworth Castle, George Gascoigne

The Fair Maid of the West. Part I and Part II. Thomas Heywood

Proserpina, Volume I and Volume II. Studies of Wayside Flowers, John Ruskin

Our Fathers Have Told Us. Part I. The Bible of Amiens. John Ruskin

The Poetry of Architecture: Or the Architecture of the Nations of Europe Considered in Its Association with Natural Scenery and National Character, John Ruskin

The Endeavour Journal of Sir Joseph Banks. Sir Joseph Banks

Christ Legends: And Other Stories, Selma Lagerlof; (trans. Velma Swanston Howard)

Chamber Music, James Joyce

Blurt, Master Constable, Thomas Middleton, Thomas Dekker

Since Yesterday, Frederick Lewis Allen

The Scholemaster: Or, Plaine and Perfite Way of Teachyng Children the Latin Tong , Roger Ascham

The Wonderful Year, 1603, Thomas Dekker

Waverley, Sir Walter Scott

Guy Mannering, Sir Walter Scott

Old Mortality, Sir Walter Scott

The Knight of Malta, John Fletcher

The Double Marriage, John Fletcher and Philip Massinger

Space Prison, Tom Godwin

The Home of the Blizzard Being the Story of the Australasian Antarctic Expedition, 1911-1914, Douglas Mawson

Wild-goose Chase , John Fletcher

If You Know Not Me, You Know Nobody. Part I and Part II, Thomas Heywood

The Ragged Trousered Philanthropists, Robert Tressell

The Island of Sheep, John Buchan

Eyes of the Woods, Joseph Altsheler

The Club of Queer Trades, G. K. Chesterton

The Financier, Theodore Dreiser

Something of Myself, Rudyard Kipling

Law of Freedom in a Platform, or True Magistracy Restored, Gerrard Winstanley

Damon and Pithias, Richard Edwards

Dido Queen of Carthage: And, The Massacre at Paris, Christopher Marlowe

Cocoa and Chocolate: Their History from Plantation to Consumer, Arthur Knapp

Lady of Pleasure, James Shirley

The South Pole: An account of the Norwegian Antarctic expedition in the "Fram," 1910-12. Volume 1 and Volume 2, Roald Amundsen

A Yorkshire Tragedy, Thomas Middleton (attrib.)

The Tragedy of Soliman and Perseda, Thomas Kyd

The Rape of Lucrece. Thomas Heywood

Myths and Legends of Ancient Greece and Rome, E. M. Berens

In the Forbidden Land, Henry Savage Arnold Landor

Across Unknown South America, by Arnold Henry Savage Landor

Illustrated History of Furniture: From the Earliest to the Present Time, Frederick Litchfield

A Narrative of Some of the Lord's Dealings with George Müller Written by Himself (Parts I-IV, 1805-1856), George Müller

The Towneley Cycle Of The Mystery Plays (Or The Wakefield Cycle): Thirty-Two Pageants, Anonymous

The Insatiate Countesse, John Marston.

Spontaneous Activity in Education, Maria Montessori.

On the Art of Writing, Sir Arthur Quiller-Couch

The Well of the Saints, J. M. Synge

Bacon's Advancement Of Learning And The New Atlantis, Francis Bacon.

Catholic Tales And Christian Songs, Dorothy Sayers.

Two Little Savages: Being the Adventures of Two Boys who Lived as Indians and What they Learned, Ernest Thompson Seton

The Sadness of Christ, Thomas More

The Family of Love, Thomas Middleton

The Passing of the Aborigines: A Lifetime Spent Among the Natives of Australia, Daisy Bates

The Children, Edith Wharton

A Record of European Armour and Arms through Seven Centuries., (Volumes I, II, III, IV and V) Francis Laking

The Book of the Farm: - Detailing The Labours Of The Farmer, Steward, Plowman, Hedger, Cattle-Man, Shepherd, Field-Worker, and Dairymaid. (Volume I), Henry Stephens

The Book of the Farm: - Detailing The Labours Of The Farmer, Steward, Plowman, Hedger, Cattle-Man, Shepherd, Field-Worker, and Dairymaid. (Volume II), Henry Stephens

The Book of the Farm: - Detailing The Labours Of The Farmer, Steward, Plowman, Hedger, Cattle-Man, Shepherd, Field-Worker, and Dairymaid. (Volume III). by Henry Stephens

The Naturalist On The River Amazons, by Henry Walter Bates.

Antarctic Penguins: A Study of their Social Habits, Dr. George Murray Levick

and many others…

Tell us what you would love to see in print again, at affordable prices!
Email: **benedictionbooks@btinternet.com**

www.ingramcontent.com/pod-product-compliance
Ingram Content Group UK Ltd.
Pitfield, Milton Keynes, MK11 3LW, UK
UKHW042017290726
14061UKWH00001BB/48